Managing the Mind

OTHER BOOKS BY DEVADATTA KĀLĪ

In Praise of the Goddess: The Devīmāhātmya and Its Meaning (2003)
The Veiling Brilliance: A Journey to the Goddess (2006)
Śvetāśvataropaniṣad: The Knowledge That Liberates (2011)

Managing the Mind

A Commonsense Guide to Patañjali's *Yogasūtra*

DEVADATTA KĀLĪ

Nicolas Hays, Inc.
Lake Worth, FL

Published in 2015 by Nicolas-Hays, Inc.
P. O. Box 540206
Lake Worth, FL 33454-0206
www.nicolashays.com

Distributed to the trade by
Red Wheel/Weiser, LLC
65 Parker St. • Ste. 7
Newburyport, MA 01950
www.redwheelweiser.com

First Edition

ISBN: 978-0-89254-212-3
Ebook: 978-0-89254- 626-8

Library of Congress Cataloging-in-Publication Data

Devadatta Kali, 1944- author.
Managing the mind : a commonsense guide to Patanjali's Yogasutra / Devadatta Kali.
pages cm
Summary: "The Yogasutra of Patanjali is described as an owner's manual for the human mind and how the mind can be used in the quest for Truth and The Managing Mind presents this most important text on Yoga and meditation in clear and straightforward English. Devadatta Kali's commentary endeavors to draw out the meaning of Patanjali's text in a coherent and modern form that will serve the real life needs of the spiritual practitioner. He has also included the original Sanskrit text for those who seek a more in-depth understanding of the hidden dimension of the Yogasutra, giving a word-by-word analysis with multiple possibilities for the meaning of the text. In addition, Devadatta Kali provides his own original interpretations of the meaning of several of the sutras. He sheds new light on their classical interpretation, which have often missed the point by overlooking the language of metaphor"— Provided by publisher.
ISBN 978-0-89254-212-3 (paperback)
1. Patañjali. Yogasutra. 2. Hindu philosophy. I. Title.
B132.Y6P24333 2015
181'.452--dc23 2015001185

Front cover and text design by David Nelson (Devadatta Kali)

Printed in the United States of America (MG)

Contents

Before You Begin vii

Chapter 1 1
Chapter 2 49
Chapter 3 95
Chapter 4 139

Selected References 169

Thematic Index by Sūtra 171

For Durgaya, Tim, and Teri
in recognition of an extraordinary friendship

Before You Begin

If you are already familiar with Patañjali's *Yogasūtra,* your first question might be, Why another version? Aren't there more than enough already? Well, maybe. But if you find, as I do, that many of them are too academic, too technical, too abstract, and not at all helpful, you might welcome a translation in straightforward English, along with a simple explanation of the realities of everyday living, the management of the mind, and the practice that leads to enlightenment. That is what this book aims to be.

I wanted to keep the language clear and simple. That said, some of the *sūtras* deal with higher states of consciousness or spiritual experience, and their explanation requires more than basic vocabulary. Even so, my aim was always to communicate as simply as the subject matter would allow.

Let's begin with three questions. Who was Patañjali? What is the *Yogasūtra?* How do we understand it?

We cannot be sure of who Patañjali was. A noted grammarian by that name lived around the third or second century BCE. More likely, our author was a different Patañjali who lived some five or six hundred years later. That probability places the *Yogasūtra* in the second or third century of the Common Era.

What is the *Yogasūtra?* This classic text is an owner's manual for the human mind. It tells us what the mind is, how it works, and how to make it work for us if we wish to reach enlightenment, Self-knowledge, or liberation. Call the goal what you will, the *Yogasūtra*'s aim is to take us there.

Many of India's ancient teaching manuals are composed in *sūtra* form. A *sūtra* ("thread") is a tightly condensed statement, sometimes only a short phrase, that may appear to have little meaning by itself. It was meant as an outline for the teacher, who would expand upon it to reveal its depth and breadth. From time to time particularly important teachers would write down their thoughts, and that is how the classical commentaries came about.

The earliest known commentary is the *Bhāṣya* by Vyāsa, who lived two or three hundred years after Patañjali. Whoever Vyāsa was—the name merely means "compiler"—he was highly influential, and our understanding of the *Yogasūtra* today may reflect his ideas more than Patañjali's own. Vācaspati Miśra, who founded a school of Advaita Vedānta in the ninth century, wrote an extensive commentary on the *Bhāṣya,* deemed only second in importance to Vyāsa's work. The fifteenth-century commentary by Vijñānabhikṣu is noteworthy for attempting to harmonize the positions of the Vedānta, Sāṁkhya, and Yoga philosophies.

But Patañjali was not interested in philosophy, at least not here. He was interested in compiling a systematic and comprehensive manual on the science and art of meditation, and in doing so he drew on a wide variety of sources. While it has become customary to think of the *Yogasūtra* as reflecting the philosophical views of the Sāṁkhya school—mainly because that was Vyāsa's perspective—that is true only in part. The *Yogasūtra*'s author was concerned primarily with what works, and he set about to present it in as universal a manner as possible.

How, then, can we know that a commentator got it right? Maybe he was more interested in promoting his own views than in trying to tell us what the *sūtras* themselves might mean. With that in mind, we should accept no commentary as the last word but instead allow the *sūtras* to inspire our own contemplation.

My aim all along was to let Patañjali's masterpiece speak for itself. There are two basic ways to interpret a text: to draw meaning out and to read meaning in. The latter usually reflects a personal perspective or bias. There are also two basic methods of scholarship: to follow the clues wherever they take you or to decide your conclusion beforehand and find the means to get there. By choosing to draw the meaning out and to follow the clues, I embarked on an adventure that was often challenging. It also produced an ample share of unexpected discoveries as things fell into place.

The format of this book is designed to serve the spiritual practitioner, whose immediate needs can be met by the English translation and the first level of commentary. For those who desire a deeper study, the original Sanskrit text is included along with a word-by-word analysis, often giving multiple possibilities of a word's meaning. Because the dictionary entry for any Sanskrit word can be a complex web of meaning-by-association, the language is often vibrantly and subtly expressive and filled with possibilities for interpretation. However, meaningful translation requires finding the best word at the proper level of discourse—at the level of basic meaning, extended meaning, or symbolic meaning. Otherwise a *sūtra* may make little or no sense.

Thirty-nine of the 195 *sūtras* have a secondary level of commentary in smaller type, addressing issues of translation and interpretation and often aimed at explaining why my interpretation departs from a traditionally accepted one. This approach may be seen as controversial, particularly among Indian scholars, who are taught to respect the earlier commentators and to accept their work as authoritative. If something seems amiss in the received tradition, the fault has to lie with the upstart who questions it and who is encouraged to find the error in his own thinking. My approach intends no disrespect for tradition but a far greater respect for Patañjali's own genius.

Most of the differences occur with *sūtras* concerned with states of consciousness that lie beyond the range of normal, everyday experience. Such *sūtras* sometimes employ the language of metaphor. To take them literally is to miss the point. The whole of Hindu teaching directs us to see the reality behind the appearance and not to be fooled by what's on the surface. The classical commentators, beginning with Vyāsa, sometimes read in sensational and fantastic powers of mind over matter where an extraordinary expansion of spiritual insight was intended. They should have recognized that. Perhaps they were seduced by images of *yogins* floating on air, whizzing through space, making themselves invisible, reading others' minds, detecting buried treasure, and self-combusting!

I must admit to finding this disturbing, not just because it strains credulity but because it compromises the excellence of Patañjali's work. By engaging in my own intensive contemplation of the *sūtras,* I began to understand that Patañjali was not describing occult powers at all but genuine mystical experiences. In the context of the *sūtras* themselves, one flowing logically into the next, a coherent, unforced, and convincing interpretation took shape, demonstrating time and again Patañjali's systematic and wholly rational method of instruction.

Is mine, then, the definitive interpretation? Of course not. Is it a valid one? I certainly hope so—one among many. There can be no last word, except that there is—but that is enlightenment itself, of which nothing can be said.

I acknowledge my deepest gratitude to two great teachers: my revered guru, Swami Prabhavananda (1893–1976) and my beloved Ma Jaya Sati Bhagavati (1940–2012).

Managing the Mind

CHAPTER 1

1.1 **Now, instruction in yoga.**

अथ योगानुशासनम् ॥

atha yogānuśāsanam

atha: now (used to announce a subject and to mark an auspicious beginning for what is to follow)
yoga: the act of joining, union, application or concentration of thought leading to Self-knowledge or liberation
anuśāsana: (further) instruction, teaching, precept, direction

Patañjali's first *sūtra* simply announces the topic, which is the teaching of yoga. At the same time, his choice of words makes clear that what he is about to share is not new or original. He has gathered together a wealth of knowledge on the long-standing practice of yoga from many different sources. He has thought deeply about all of it and is about to present his findings, step by step, in a clear and logical way.

The word *anuśāsana* means "further teaching" and implies an already existing body of knowledge. Through this single word Patañjali acknowledges his indebtedness to the traditions that preceded him.

Yoga was already practiced in the Indus Valley at least forty-five hundred years ago. Carved images found there depict a male figure, thought to be Śiva, seated in a meditative or yogic posture. The earliest verbal record is a hymn from the Ṛgveda (10.136) describing a long-haired, naked devotee of Rudra (Śiva) who bears a striking resemblance to *yogins* today. Later, the Kaṭhopaniṣad and the Śvetāśvataropaniṣad (ca. 500 BCE) offer somewhat developed accounts of yogic practice, although they appear rudimentary in light of Patañjali's later work. The Bhagavadgītā presents a variety of yogic disciplines involving knowledge, action, devotion, and meditation, while the Tantric *Pāśupatasūtra* presents a highly structured yoga with eight limbs that bear the same names Patañjali would use later. Meditation and yoga were widely practiced in ancient India, and knowledge was commonly exchanged among the ancestors of today's Hindus, Buddhists, and Jains before sectarian boundaries became firmly drawn.

1.2 **Yoga is the stilling of the mind's activity.**

योगश्चित्तवृत्तिनिरोधः ॥

yogaś cittavṛttinirodhaḥ

yoga: discipline leading to Self-knowledge or liberation
citta: mind (with its functions of perceiving, thinking, imagining, intending, deciding, memory, and self-definition)
vṛtti: activity, function, modification, fluctuation, "thought-wave"
nirodha: restraint, check, control, stilling

Now that the teacher has announced his topic, the next step is to explain what yoga is. Many different kinds of practice go by that name. A popular form of yoga has to do with postures that promote physical, mental, and spiritual well-being, but this is not what Patañjali is about to teach. His classic form of yoga is the science of managing the mind. Its aim is to instruct in meditation and to lead toward Self-knowledge, enlightenment, or liberation.

It is important to keep in mind that yoga is both the *method* and the *goal*. Yoga is both the way to quiet the activity of the mind and the state of enlightenment and freedom that shines forth once the mind becomes completely still.

What is the mind? As Patañjali understands it, the mind is a person's own field of awareness, through which he or she experiences life in this world. The mind receives, sorts, and processes the information that comes to it through the senses of hearing, touch, sight, taste, and smell. It compares and reasons, and at the end of the process it reaches a conclusion. Along the way it also personalizes the experience. It is *I* who hear and see and think and decide and know. Whatever is present to the mind becomes *mine:* my experience, my idea, my opinion, my decision, my memory.

Getting to the state where all this mental activity stops means going beyond everyday states of mind. The commentator Vyāsa noted that the mind has five degrees or levels of activity. It can be overly excited, unable to focus, jumping restlessly from one thing to another. Or it can fall into a heavy dullness of the "I can hardly think" variety. Between these extremes there is the normal state of awareness where the mind focuses on one thing for a while, then wanders off to something else until yet another thought arises or something else claims its attention. In other words, the usual state of the mind involves a certain amount of distraction.

Is that ordinary state good enough to bring lasting peace and satisfaction? Obviously not. So Vyāsa describes a fourth level, where attention becomes one-pointed. Focusing on one thing and one thing only is the way to still the restlessness of the mind, and it is the guiding principle throughout all the phases of yoga. Patañjali will show how concentration can be deepened and prolonged all the way to the final goal, the fifth level of awareness, where all mental activity ceases.

The five states of awareness are not found in the *Yogasūtra* itself but come from Vyāsa's commentary on the first *sūtra*. They are listed as *kṣipta* ("scattered," "highly stimulated"), *mūḍha* ("stupefied," "lethargic"), *vikṣipta* ("alternately steady and distracted"), *ekāgra* ("one-pointed," "focused"), and *niruddha* ("restrained," "held in check," "stilled"). The first four apply to states of ordinary awareness. The fifth describes the state of yoga.

The word *yoga* is related to the English work *yoke,* which means to join together. The different schools of Hindu thought understand the term in different ways. According to the nondualist philosophy of Advaita Vedānta, *yoga* means the union or merging of the individual conscious self (*ātman*) with the infinite Self, the transcendental Brahman. In contrast, the dualistic Sāṁkhya philosophy recognizes two eternally separate realities—consciousness (*puruṣa*) and materiality (*prakṛti*). According to Sāṁkhya, *yoga* may be the union of the individual's awareness with its own true nature as consciousness, but reaching that state involves the *disunion* or *disengagement* of the essential conscious being (*puruṣa*) from the defining and binding characteristics of material nature (*prakṛti*) with which it has seemingly become entangled and consequently formed a mistaken sense of identity.

Following Vyāsa, the prevailing opinion is that Patañjali subscribed to the Sāṁkhya philosophy. In truth, Patañjali's own philosophical views are not known and are almost irrelevant. What matters is that his masterly synthesis of yogic practice works.

1.3 **To experience this is to abide in one's own essential nature.**

तदा द्रष्टुः स्वरूपेऽवस्थानम् ॥

tadā draṣṭuḥ svarūpe 'vasthānam

tadā: then
draṣṭṛ: one who sees, one who experiences
svarūpa: one's own nature
avasthāna: an abiding, a taking of one's place, a condition

When all the distracting and overshadowing activity of the mind ceases, then only consciousness itself remains. The light of consciousness—the real Self—shines forth, unchanging. This state of illumination, enlightenment, Self-knowledge, or liberation is the boundless joy of one's own true being. It can be experienced but never described. We call it a state, but that word means "condition," and the Self is free of any condition and beyond anything that can affect it or define it in any way.

It is what it is—pure awareness, aware of itself alone, and that is beyond the power of thought or speech to express.

1.4 **Otherwise one identifies with the mind's activities.**

वृत्तिसारूप्यमितरत्र ॥

vṛttisārūpyam itaratra

vṛtti: activity, fluctuation, or modification of the mind
sārūpya: sameness, similarity of form, conformity with
itaratra: otherwise

A person who is not enlightened will remain in the ordinary state of awareness, living in the world as an individual and unique personality. The human mind, caught up in the ever-changing panorama before it, interacts with what it experiences, identifying with some of it, resisting other parts of it, and knowing little rest.

This is not to say that the light of the true Self has ceased to shine. This human personality is illumined by it; otherwise, how could we even be aware that we exist? What Patañjali tells us is that there are two ways to experience consciousness: either as the unchanging, self-luminous Self or as the finite individual caught up in a dynamic world of "I and other."

1.5 **The activities are five-fold; they are troubling or not.**

वृत्तयः पञ्चतय्यः क्लिष्टाक्लिष्टाः ॥

vṛttayaḥ pañcatayyaḥ kliṣṭākliṣṭāḥ

vṛtti: activity, fluctuation, or modification of the mind
pañcatayya: fivefold
kliṣṭa: afflicted, connected to pain or suffering, causing pain
akliṣṭa: untroubled, undistressed, not painful, not causing pain

The mind is never totally at rest but always engaged in some sort of activity. Patañjali recognizes five kinds of mental activity, which he will name in the next *sūtra*. For now he notes that *any* of them can be either troubling or untroubling, either positive or negative, either detrimental or beneficial.

Patañjali uses the terms *kliṣṭa* and *akliṣṭa*. The first can mean painful," "troubling," "distressing," "harmful," or "detrimental." The second indicates the opposite but is rarely translated in positive terms. Instead we find *akliṣṭa* rendered as "not painful" or "non-afflicted" more often than as "pleasant" or "benign." This choice may reflect the outlook of the Sāṁkhya philosophy, which emphasizes the suffering (*duḥkha*) inherent in life and presents its knowledge-based teaching as a way to permanent release from the pain-laden human condition. It should be noted, however, that overall Patañjali appears to be more matter-of-fact than pessimistic. To reiterate his essential point, any of the five kinds of mental activity he is about to name can be pain-bearing or not.

1.6 **They are right knowledge, misapprehension, ideation, sleep, and memory.**

प्रमाणविपर्ययविकल्पनिद्रास्मृतयः ॥

pramāṇaviparyayavikalpanidrāsmṛtayaḥ

pramāṇa: right knowledge, valid cognition
viparyaya: misapprehension, misperception, error, mistake
vikalpa: ideation, conceptualization, imagination
nidrā: sleep
smṛti: memory, recollection

We are introduced here to a pattern that will be characteristic of Patañjali's teaching. In one *sūtra* he will give a list of terms, and then he will explain them, one at a time, in the *sūtras* that immediately follow.

Everything that we experience in life, we experience through the mind. Whatever happens around us, whatever thoughts and feelings arise within, whatever we dream for the future or recollect from the past—all that is a result of the mind's activity, which falls into five basic categories.

Any mental activity can be positive or negative. Let's take the case of right knowledge. In general right knowledge seems to be a good thing. There's satisfaction in "getting it right." But what if that right knowledge brings bad news? Then it is painful. What about wrong knowledge? Maybe someone will tell a lie to shield you from a painful truth. Is that positive or negative? Or let's say you've made a mistake in your finances and think you have more money than you actually do. As long as that misapprehension lasts, you're happy. And what about ideation, the ability to form concepts or to imagine? The mind conjures up pleasant daydreams, but just as easily it creates anxieties. In sleep also you might have a pleasant dream or a nightmare. And then there are the memories of the past that surface now and then, bringing joy, wistfulness, regret, resentment, or a host of other emotions.

1.7 **The means of right knowledge are direct perception, inference, and reliable authority.**

प्रत्यक्षानुमानागमाः प्रमाणानि ॥

pratyakṣānumānāgamaḥ pramāṇāni

pratyakṣa: direct perception
anumāna: inference
āgama: reliable authority, a body of traditionally accepted doctrine or sacred teaching
pramāṇa: correct knowledge

The first of the mind's five activities is right knowledge. Patañjali says that it rests on three means of knowing. The primary means is direct experience. The five channels of perception—hearing, touch, sight, smell, and taste—stream information into the mind, which receives it and tries to make sense of it. At the end of the process, I know what I see—the apple tree in the garden. I know what I hear—the rustling of its leaves. I know what I feel—the smooth, round firmness of its fruit. I know what I smell—the apple's delightful fragrance. I know what I taste—its distinctive flavor. I do not doubt my own experience.

The second means of right knowledge is inference. Something allows me to know something about something I do not perceive directly. Where there is smoke, there is fire. I do not actually see the fire but can reason from the sight or smell of the smoke that there is a fire. The smoke is the clue. The internal workings of the mind take over from there and allow me to draw a correct conclusion.

The third means of right knowledge rests apart from the other two. What if there is no opportunity to perceive directly or to figure something out on the basis of evidence? I have to rely on someone to tell me. Let's say an event happens halfway around the world. I am not there, I do not witness it, and I have no hint that it even took place. Yet I learn about it from a trustworthy source and accept it as true. In terms of spiritual teaching, the sacred texts of a religion are held to be a trustworthy source or reliable authority, and what they convey is knowledge about the highest truth of our being.

For now it is important to recognize that Patañjali is talking about the five activities of the mind in the here and now. We must not mistake right knowledge for absolute truth.

1.8 **Misapprehension is false knowledge, based on an appearance at odds with reality.**

विपर्ययो मिथ्याज्ञानमतद्रूपप्रतिष्ठम् ॥

viparyayo mithyājñānam atadrūpapratiṣṭham

viparyaya: misapprehension, misperception, error, mistake
mithyā: false, deceptive, untrue
jñāna: knowledge
atad: not that, other than what it appears to be
rūpa: form, appearance
pratiṣṭha: basis, foundation

Living in this world, we sometimes get things right, and sometimes we get them wrong. The unavoidable companion of right knowledge is misapprehension or error. Take our perceptions, for example. Occasionally the mind misinterprets the information it receives through the senses. A classic example is seeing a gnarled tree trunk in the semidarkness and mistaking it for a human figure. Or take the reasoning process. We can and do make mistakes in our thinking. Often a mistake is honest, but we are not immune to kidding ourselves either, because of what we want to believe. We engage in self-deception or denial and then even kid ourselves that we're not doing it! In all these instances there is a disconnect between what actually is and how we understand it to be. Such thinking is at odds with reality.

What is reality? Some schools of Indian thought believe that this world is an illusion, but that is not a universal opinion. Patañjali recognizes the higher reality of the Self along with the reality of this world. *Sūtras* 1.3 and 1.4 tell us that we experience one or the other—either the self-aware Self in its own pristine clarity or this ever-moving world of the here and now, where we are subject to right knowledge as well as to error.

1.9 **Ideation rests on verbal knowledge apart from a perceived object.**

शब्दज्ञानानुपाती वस्तुशून्यो विकल्पः ॥

śabdajñānānupātī vastuśūnyo vikalpaḥ

śabda: sound, word, speech, language, verbal communication
jñāna: knowledge
anupātin: following as a consequence or result
vastu: object, thing
śūnya: empty, void
vikalpa: ideation, imagination, thinking, conceptualization

Through the process of inference the mind can reason and draw conclusions. Only a sign hinting at something else, such as the presence of smoke, is needed. Now we learn that even when an object or an event is not physically present, we can still think about it. If the stimulus is no longer an external object or event, it can be something internal and purely mental—an idea of something remembered from our own experience or an idea of something created purely by our own mind.

The mind has great creative power. The power to create ideas has many names, depending on the nature of what it creates. When the ideas are abstract, we speak of conceptualization. When something unexpected and visionary comes to mind, we speak of imagination or inspiration. Without the ability to ideate we would not have any of our arts, sciences, and other human achievements.

1.10 **Sleep is mental activity based on the awareness of nothingness.**

अभावप्रत्ययालम्बना वृत्तिर्निद्रा ॥

abhāvapratyayālambanā vṛttir nidrā

abhāva: nonexistence, absence
pratyaya: idea, conception, anything present to awareness
ālambana: foundation, substratum
vṛtti: activity, function, occupation with, mode of conduct
nidrā: sleep

While we are awake, the body and the mind work together as a single unit—as a person with a personality. When we sleep, the mind disengages from the body and the outer world, but its power of ideation continues to be active in creating dreams.

In a dream, just as when you are awake, you are the central character of your world. But now the world is one of your own making and exists only in your own mind. The dream may be realistic or fantastic. Someone who sees you sleeping has no idea of your dream, but you experience it as vividly as if you were awake. Sometimes the effect of a dream will persist even after you wake up.

What about when you sleep soundly and do not dream? That is the subject of this *sūtra*. Even then the mind retains some measure of activity. You wake up refreshed and say, "I slept well. I knew nothing." That's just the point: dreamless sleep is mental activity—awareness of what we call nothing.

Think about that simple statement, "I knew nothing." The sense of self is there (I), it did something (knew), and that mental activity had an object (nothing). There is a threefold division of knower, knowing, and known. The mind was aware of all three, but because mental activity never ceased, you were *not* aware of your true being as self-luminous, self-aware consciousness.

There is a message here: for all the apparent stillness, deep sleep is not yoga.

1.11 **Memory is the retention of past experiences.**

अनुभूतविषयासंप्रमोषः स्मृतिः ॥

anubhūtaviṣayāsaṁpramoṣaḥ smṛtiḥ

anubhūta: that which is experienced, perceived
viṣaya: object, subject matter, content
asaṁpramoṣa: not allowing to be dropped (from memory)
smṛti: memory

Whatever we experience, we experience it through the mind. Whatever comes before the mind may seem fleeting—here one moment, gone the next—but in fact everything leaves a lasting impression. Patañjali will have much more to say about these subconscious impressions later on. There is no way to imagine the number of such impressions stored in the mind, but they are all there below the surface, ready to spring back to life at a moment's notice.

The four kinds of mental activity already described—right knowledge, misapprehension, ideation, and sleep—all add constantly to this vast store of impressions. Every time we have been right or wrong has left its mark. Everything imagined or dreamed, even the experience of deep sleep, is imprinted on the subconscious mind. It all becomes part of who we are. Each one of us is the sum total of our past experience, and every person is unique. We are conditioned by all our experiences, and these form our character, for better or worse.

Memory is present in every act of knowing. Information streams in constantly through the five senses, and the mind tries to make sense of it all. First it compares the new data with its stored impressions. A small child, encountering an apple for the first time, doesn't know what it is, has no name for it, and maybe rolls it on the ground, thinking it might be a plaything. The child is told that it is called an apple and that it is good to eat. That information enters the storehouse of the mind and resurfaces every time an apple is present.

This principle works not just with acts of perception but with every other kind of knowing, no matter how concrete or abstract, how simple or complex. All those stored impressions of things and people and events and words and ideas can spring back to our present awareness at a moment's notice.

An understanding of what memory is and how it works plays an important role in yogic practice. We learned at the outset that yoga is the stilling of the mind's activity. Since remembering activates our subconscious impressions, we will need to learn how to stop this from happening.

In fact, there are three levels of practice, called gross, subtle, and causal. The first is the stilling of perceptions. This relates to things outside of us in the surrounding world. The second is the stilling of intellectual activity. This has to do with ideas present in the inner realm of the mind. The third is the prevention of subconscious impressions from even arising.

Here it is important to understand that yoga is not about repression. Rather, it is about cultivating an equanimity that leaves the impressions powerless to affect us. We will explore these meditative practices later on.

1.12 **The stilling of these [five activities] arises through repeated endeavor and dispassion.**

अभ्यासवैराग्याभ्यां तन्निरोधः ॥

abhyāsavairāgyābhyāṁ tannirodhaḥ

abhyāsa: pratice; especially continuous, repeated endeavor
vairāgya: dispassion, freedom from desire, detachment
tad: these (the five-fold mental activity)
nirodha: restraint, check, control

The answer to stilling the mind's activities lies in two principles: repeated endeavor and dispassion. The first is continuous, persistent practice—discipline, diligence, and perseverance. In plain language, keeping at it. The second principle is dispassion. All those sensations, feelings, thoughts, opinions, and ideas that come before the mind—do you let them push your buttons or pull your strings? Or do you remain calm even in the face of distressing circumstances?

Patañjali mentions these two principles of repeated endeavor and dispassion in the same breath. Why? Because the two work hand in hand. To cite the classic illustration, you can row a boat throughout the night, but if you did not lift the anchor, you will be in exactly the same place when morning comes. Or, you can lift the anchor and decide not to row. Then you merely drift and could end up anywhere.

Each principle provides balance for the other. Practice requires the exercise of will, but that can have its pitfalls. You have to work diligently to achieve any goal, but it is easy to become so caught up with an endeavor, so identified with it, and so possessive of it that *it* takes hold of *you*. The more emotionally invested you become, the more subject you are to the ups and downs of success and failure. This is where dispassion brings balance. Dispassion is about not getting attached and not allowing events or circumstances to disturb your inner well-being. At the same time it is important to remember that dispassion is not indifference. Indifference is not caring. If you didn't care, why would you try at all? Dispassion allows you to be diligent in the right way.

Together practice and dispassion can serve us well in daily

living. In spiritual life, they become potent tools for quieting the mind and enabling us to advance toward enlightenment.

1.13 **Of these [two], repeated endeavor is the effort [to remain] in steadiness.**

तत्र स्थितौ यत्नोऽभ्यासः ॥

tatra sthitau yatno 'bhyāsaḥ

tatra: there, of these
sthiti: steadiness, stability
yatna: exertion, effort
abhyāsa: pratice; especially continuous, repeated endeavor

The mind is constantly in motion. Even in deep sleep there is some level of activity. While we are awake and interacting with our surroundings, the mind's normal state is to be distracted. Attention turns here and there, to one thing after another. Even if there is little going on and we think we can be quiet, it doesn't happen. In those moments we become aware of the mind's internal chatter as thought after thought rises up.

The way to stop the movement of a physical object is to hold it steady. The same principle holds true when the object is the activity of the mind. The way to check the fluctuations that arise from external sources or internally is to direct the attention to a single thought and to keep it there—to make the mind one-pointed. If the mind can be held in steadiness on one thought alone, it will no longer jump about. There still will be activity of a sort, but it will be singularly focused and subdued.

1.14 **Now over time, when cultivated attentively, respectfully, and without interruption, this [endeavor] becomes firmly grounded.**

स तु दीर्घकालनैरन्तर्यसत्कारासेवितो दृढभूमिः ॥

sa tu dīrghakālanairantaryasatkārāsevito dṛḍhabhūmiḥ

sa: it (endeavor)
tu: now (emphatic)
dīrgha: long
kāla: time
nairantarya: without interruption, continually
satkāra: honor, virtue, reverence, respect
āsevita: practiced assiduously
dṛḍha: firm
bhūmi: ground

Patañjali tells us not to expect a quick fix. How many years have you *not* disciplined your mind? Do you think that can change overnight? The practice of yoga is a long-term commitment, to be done regularly and consistently. It is all too easy to slip back into old habits, so practice means establishing a routine and keeping to it.

A key to success lies in the word *respect*. If we take our practice seriously, we recognize the value of what we are doing. With that respectful attitude, steady commitment is not so hard after all.

The Sanskrit word for repeated endeavor contains also the idea of cumulative effect. Practice adds up. The more you practice, the better you become at it. The better you become, the easier it gets. It is no longer something you force yourself to do but that you look forward to doing. As the results begin to show, you become firmly grounded.

1.15 **Dispassion is the consummate knowledge [that arises] with the freedom from desire for anything perceived or even heard about.**

दृष्टानुश्रविकविषयवितृष्णस्य वशीकारसंज्ञा वैराग्यम् ॥

dṛṣṭānuśravikaviṣayavitṛṣṇasya vaśīkārasaṁjñā vairāgyam

dṛṣṭa: that which is seen (or more broadly, experienced through any of the five senses)

anuśravika: heard repeatedly, transmitted orally from person to person
viṣaya: object, subject matter, content
vitṛṣṇa: freedom from desire, satisfaction
vaśīkāra: mastery
saṁjñā: clear knowledge or understanding
vairāgya: dispassion, freedom from desire, detachment

Every experience is stored in the form of a mental impression, and those impressions rise to the surface in connection with new experiences and play a role in how we act and react. The conditioning of the mind causes us to reach out towards some things and to pull back from others. This principle of attraction and aversion drives us in all we think and do.

Let's suppose you are fond of apples and one is placed before you. You see it, anticipate its juicy freshness, and want to eat it. Now let's suppose you can't stand apples. If one is set before you, your urge may be to push it away. In either case, you react to your direct perception.

If no apple is present, just hearing the word *apple* may be enough to set your mouth watering. Or to make you shudder. There is no direct experience of the apple, but merely hearing about it is enough to trigger a response. We are all conditioned beings. Food is just one example. We react—sometimes very strongly—to objects, people, other living creatures, events, situations, and ideas.

Dispassion is the freedom from reaction *and* a lessening of mental activity. If you decide not to react, that places *you* in control of your thoughts and feelings—not someone or something else. Rather than being torn this way and that, you remain serene. That is why dispassion is such an important part of yogic practice.

1.16 **The supreme [dispassion], arising from a glimpse of the Self, is the quenching of thirst for any definable thing.**

तत्परं पुरुषख्यातेर्गुणवैतृष्ण्यम् ॥

tatparaṁ puruṣakhyāter guṇavaitṛṣṇyam

tad: that (dispassion)
para: higher, superior, supreme
puruṣa: spirit or consciousness, unrelated to anything else and ever unchanging; the true Self
khyāti: perception, knowledge, view, idea
guṇa: quality, fundamental constituent of nature
vaitṛṣṇya: quenching of thirst, freedom from desire

Dispassion creates a new frame of reference for looking at life. As we become more and more grounded in this perspective, we see things in a different way. The mind becomes immune to the influences that once colored our attitudes, and new clarity begins to emerge.

Our exercise of dispassion has to do with how we relate to the things of this world—to the disturbing or not disturbing, to suffering and well-being, to pain and pleasure. As we become increasingly immune to their effects, we begin to go beyond this play of opposites. What I like or don't like belongs to the small, ego-self with which I no longer identify so strongly. As the ego loses its grip and the mind comes to greater quietude, I begin to have a larger sense of being that goes beyond the limits of my personality. Fleeting glimpses of my higher Self evoke a sense of wonder and offer a foretaste of what still lies ahead.

1.17 **[The endeavor to still the mind is called] cognitive when the focusing of thought, insight, joy, and one's own sense of self are [all] present.**

वितर्कविचारानन्दास्मितारूपानुगमात्संप्रज्ञातः ॥

vitarkavicārānandāsmitārūpānugamāt saṁprajñātaḥ

vitarka: the initial direction of the mind toward an object of thought, the taking hold of an object of thought, the application of thought, applied thought
vicāra: continued attentiveness toward the object along with a deepening appreciation of its associations and meanings

ānanda: happiness, enjoyment, joy
asmitā: "I-am-ness," egoity, sense of the personal self
rūpa: appearance
anugama: conformity, accordance
saṁprajñāta: cognitive, denoting a state of concentration accompanied by various kinds of mental activity

Yoga is both the practice and the goal; it covers the whole spectrum of experience from our initial attempts to the ultimate realization. Insight unfolds one level at a time in a logical, methodical way, owing to the nature of the mind and its workings. This *sūtra* is concerned with that gradual process.

In ordinary awareness attention shifts from one thing to another and another—and another. Real attention rarely lasts for long, and even then it may not be all that deep or full. We strive for a higher range of awareness, described as one-pointed. Note the word *range.* One-pointedness is focus on a single thing, but even here the *degree* of concentration varies. It may be shallow and short-lived, and before long we're back to the usual mental wandering. With repeated effort our concentration may grow deeper and longer-lasting. Persisting in our attempt to hold the mind steady, we eventually reach a state of awareness beyond anything in our normal, everyday experience.

This *sūtra* may seem a bit technical, so let's take it one word at a time. The word *cognitive* means "having to do with the processes of knowing or perceiving." This means that from the very beginning, meditation needs an object, a point of focus for the mind. "The focusing of thought" means directing attention to a particular object and holding it there.

Let's say the object you've chosen is the sky. It's a good choice, because the sky is something you can see. Now with your eyes closed, as you try to hold your attention to *the thought of the sky,* other ideas crop up. You might think of clouds drifting by. Already your mind has been diverted from the thought of the sky itself. Clouds are not the sky. And then those thoughts of clouds give rise to other associations, and only some time later do you become aware that you have forgotten all about the sky. So, you bring the mind back and try again. This is how it goes in the early stages, because the mind's natural tendency is to wander.

When you succeed in stilling all the other thoughts and fix your attention on the thought of the sky alone, your mind remains active, but now the activity is one of continuing attentiveness, not wandering. Thoughts still arise, but they have to do with a deeper understanding of the sky.

One result of such penetrating insight is that the mind becomes quiet enough for you to feel an underlying joy. This joy has been present all along, because it belongs to your true nature. You've just been too distracted to notice it before.

But you still have a long way to go. Your own sense of existence as an individual remains. You are aware that it is you who are sitting there, trying to quiet your mind by holding it to one and only one thought.

Patañjali uses the word *cognitive* to describe this range of awareness. This simply means that three factors are present: the small you as the knower, the object of meditation as the known, and the process of knowing that relates the two. To put it another way, the early phases of concentration are not all that different from your ordinary way of thinking.

Much misunderstanding surrounds this *sūtra*. First, the grammatical subject is *samprajñāta,* an adjective meaning "the cognitive [one]." The cognitive what? Vyāsa supposed that the missing noun was *samādhi,* the state of meditative union, but so far Patañjali has not even mentioned that word. Would he, who has been so careful to introduce and explain every term and concept, suddenly jump ahead to an advanced state of consciousness without even naming it? *Samprajñāta* must modify a noun of the masculine gender that has already been mentioned. That noun is *abhyāsa,* found in *sūtras* 1.12–14, where it is defined as the effort to remain in steadiness. The present *sūtra* is about holding the cognitive processes in steadiness. Indeed, the very next *sūtra* confirms that the unmentioned noun is *abhyāsa:* "Following upon the conscious effort (*abhyāsa*) to still all thought … ."

Interpretation of the terms *vitarka, vicāra, ānanda,* and *asmitā* also has given rise to misunderstanding. The first three are found together, in the same order, in Buddhist teaching. In that light, the meaning of the *sūtra* becomes immediately clear. *Vitarka* means initially directing the mind toward a particular object and holding it there. *Vicāra* means the continued exercise of the mind on that object alone along with a dawning awareness of its properties and nature. The insight of *vicāra* can give rise to *ānanda,* or joy. The classic illustration is that *vitarka* is like taking hold of a pot and *vicāra* is like scrubbing it clean to remove all accumulated matter so it can shine. *Ānanda* refers to the joy of beholding its inherent luster.

The fourth word, *asmitā,* does not figure in the Buddhist teaching but is essential to Patañjali's yoga. Its literal translation is "I-amness." It means the conventional sense of selfhood—I as my individual personality. At the lower states of cognitive effort, the individual self is present as a participant in the process.

The classical commentators, following Vyāsa, assumed that Patañjali was speaking at this juncture about *samādhi*—advanced meditative absorption. They took the terms *vitarka, vicāra, ānanda,* and *asmitā* as describing four degrees of *samprajñāta samādhi,* which they called *savitarka, savicāra, sānanda,* and *sāsmitā,* but they failed to agree on what those are. (For a detailed analysis, see Edwin F. Bryant, *The Yoga Sūtras of Patañjali,* pp. 61–70.) Later commentators jumped ahead to *sūtras* 1.42–44, plucked the terms *nirvitarka* and *nirvicāra* out of context, and came up with six degrees of lower *samādhi,* only adding to the confusion.

1.18 **Following upon the conscious effort to still all thought, there is a further [state in which only] latent impressions [remain stored in the mind].**

विरामप्रत्ययाभ्यासपूर्वः संस्कारशेषोऽन्यः ॥

virāmapratyayābhyāsapūrvaḥ saṁskāraśeṣo 'nyaḥ

virāma: cessation, termination, silencing
pratyaya: idea, conception, anything present to awareness
abhyāsa: continuous practice, persistent endeavor, diligence
pūrva: preceded by
saṁskāra: impression

śeṣa: residue
anya: other, different, additional, further

Once you have managed to quiet the conscious mind so that there is no discernible activity, you must not be lulled into thinking you've attained the final goal. Below the surface rests a vast storehouse of past experience in the form of latent impressions, lying in wait to rise up from the subconscious and set the mind back into motion. As long as these are present, liberation cannot occur.

Here Vyāsa compounds the error. Along with his misconstrued concept of *samprajñāta samādhi,* he now takes the word *anya* ("other") to mean *asamprajñāta samādhi,* the ultimate state of non-cognitive absorption. However, this *sūtra* does not describe any such state, but rather a state in which latent impressions *still remain stored in the mind.* Patañjali simply calls this *another* state. Moreover the term *asamprajñata* occurs nowhere in the *Yogasūtra.* It is Vyāsa's own creation. Patañjali's own term for the highest meditative union is *nirbīja samādhi,* which won't appear until the last *sūtra* of this chapter.

1.19 **[Because of those impressions] the idea of rebirth [persists even] for the deceased, whose dissolution is in nature [and not in consciousness].**

भवप्रत्ययो विदेहप्रकृतिलयानाम् ॥

bhavapratyayo videhaprakṛtilayānām

bhava: becoming, existence
pratyaya: idea, conception, anything present to awarensss
videha: dead, deceased, bodiless, incorporeal
prakṛti: nature, the material principle and its manifestations
laya: dissolution

To show how persistent those impressions are, Patañjali mentions that even the dead cannot get free of them. Even after the soul leaves the body and the body dissolves back into the natural elements that it was made of, the accumulated impressions adhere to the soul and set the conditions for its next birth.

Commentators have read a great deal into this *sūtra,* taking it to refer to various classes of advanced *yogins,* celestial beings, or disincarnate gods who inhabit subtle dimensions. A straightforward reading shows no need for that.

1.20 **For others, [those who still live, the stilling of the mind results] from firm conviction, vigor, mindfulness, meditative absorption, and insight.**

श्रद्धावीर्यस्मृतिसमाधिप्रज्ञापूर्वक इतरेषाम् ॥

śraddhāvīryasmṛtisamādhiprajñāpūrvaka itareṣām

śraddhā: conviction born of experience, faith
vīrya: vigor, vitality, potency, power
smṛti: memory, recollection
samādhi: union with or absorption into that which is contemplated in deep meditation
prajñā: wisdom, insight
pūrvaka: preceded by, following upon, resulting from
itara: other

Two *sūtras* ago we learned that it is possible in this lifetime to reach a state of consciousness where all mental activity has been stilled until only the subconscious baggage hangs on. Now Patañjali introduces five factors that lead toward that ever deepening quietude. They are firm conviction, vigor, mindfulness, mental absorption, and insight.

Once you have begun to see some results from your practice, you develop a conviction born of your own experience. The word for that conviction is often translated as "faith," but it means more than belief in what you are told. It is something you have proven to yourself, and it carries the stamp of authenticity that will inspire you to keep moving forward.

Vigor comes from the proper and efficient use of the mind's

already present energy. By not frittering it away on trivial matters or wasting it on jumping from one thought to another, you have a greater reserve of it to direct consciously toward ever-increasing stillness.

Mindfulness is using the memory in the best possible way, to keep the practice and goal of yoga ever present.

Absorption is the level of complete and undeviating concentration that brings us close to the ultimate goal. It lies just before the state of full enlightenment. Even an instant of such absorption will validate and reinforce our resolve.

Insight is right understanding. In this life not everything is as it appears to be, but insight—a purified and enhanced state of awareness—enables us to discern the truth behind the appearances, especially the truth of our own being.

1.21 **It is near for those whose determination is ardent.**

तिव्रसंवेगानामासन्नः ॥

tīvrasaṁvegānām āsannaḥ

tīvra: strong, intense, ardent
saṁvega: excitement, desire for liberation, determinaton
āsanna: near, proximate, reached, obtained

The more determined you are to succeed, the faster you should expect to succeed, because determination will intensify your practice. That said, you should never feel grimly determined. Gritting the teeth is not the way to peace or joy or to the expansion of self into Self. Consider Patañjali's advice: ardent enthusiasm is the proper frame of mind.

1.22 **Even so, there are differences [in the degree of ardor] from mild to moderate to beyond measure.**

मृदुमध्याधिमात्रत्वात्ततोऽपि विशेषः ॥

mṛdumadhyādhimātratvāt tato 'pi viśeṣaḥ

mṛdu: mild, slight
madhya: moderate
adhimātratva: excessive, above measure
tatas: there
api: and, also, moreover, surely, assuredly
viśeṣa: characteristic difference, differentiation

No two people are alike, and yoga is not a one-size-fits-all proposition. Each person's journey will take a different route and proceed at a different pace. That said, this *sūtra* should be a reminder to keep an eye on our own sense of commitment. Is my sincerity something that waxes and wanes? Do I want to establish a regular routine for meditation and can I keep to it, even it if means giving up something else? Do I want to devote myself whole-heartedly to my practice to the point where it becomes the very center of my life?

1.23 **Then again, [stillness may arise] from profound contemplation of the Supreme Being.**

ईश्वरप्रणिधानाद्वा ॥

īśvarapraṇidhānād vā

īśvara: lord, master, the Deity, God (the term has various meanings in the different schools of Indian thought)
praṇidhāna: directing one's thoughts to, profound contemplation, dedication, reverence, devotion
vā: or, possibly, optionally

So far Patañjali has taught us about the mind, how it works, and how to direct it toward Self-knowledge, enlightenment, and liberation. We might think that yoga is purely a kind of psychological enterprise.

Now he brings in God.

Or does he? Everyone has an idea of who or what God is or is not. That was as true in Patañjali's time as it is today. And so the word he uses is a fairly neutral term often found in philosophical writings and best translated here as "Supreme

Being." It may be that Patañjali does not wish to impose any sectarian understanding of God but to leave the matter open to broad interpretation.

In light of Vyāsa's commentary, it is generally assumed that Patañjali's Yoga has its philosophical basis in Sāṁkhya. While there are similarities, there are also marked differences, and perhaps the most notable one is that the *Yogasūtra* allows for God whereas the Sāṁkhya system is usually characterized as atheistic. (For more on this question, see Gerald James Larson's *Classical Sāṁkhya* and Andrew J. Nicholson's *Unifying Hinduism.*)

Our immediate concern is what *īśvara* might mean here. Its basic meaning is "lord," "master," "God," "the Supreme Being," or "the supreme soul." India's religious traditions hold various conceptions of divinity reflecting three philosophical points of view. The dualistic (*dvaita*) position maintains that God and the human soul are eternally distinct. The schools of qualified nondualism (*viśiṣṭādvaita*) or unity-in-difference (*bhedābheda*) hold that God and the soul, while separate, are of the same substance, such as fire and its sparks. The nondualistic (*advaita*) position is that God and the soul are ultimately one—the singular, transcendent reality of pure consciousness. This is stated succinctly in the great Upaniṣadic dictum *ayam ātmā brahma* ("This self is Brahman").

The classical commentators go to great lengths to fashion interpretations of the *sūtras* involving *īśvara* that will accord with their own religious and philosophical doctrines. (See Bryant, pp. 81–99.) However, it is important to keep in mind that some of those doctrines were formulated centuries after Patañjali's time and contain ideas that would have been unknown to him. Moreover, the *Yogasūtra* gives us no indication of Patañjali's own religious views. If this text is indeed the synthesis of knowledge that its author proclaims it to be (*atha yogāṇuśāsanam*), it represents no single philosophical or theological view. We must simply accept that the matter of *īśvara* is open to interpretation.

The other term, *praṇidhāna,* is often taken in the sense of religious devotion, dedication, or even submission—connotations that do not appear in Monier-Williams's dictionary. There, *praṇidhāna* is literally "a setting down before" and by extension "respectful conduct," "attention paid," "profound religious meditation," or "abstract contemplation." Rather than any superficial idea of devotion to God as found in popular religion, Patañjali's *īśvarapraṇidhāna* carries the meaning of a respectful, dedicated, and profound mindfulness of the divine presence.

1.24 **The Supreme Being is an aspect of consciousness untouched by [any] store of impressions that ripen into action and cause distress.**

क्लेशकर्मविपाकाशयैरपरामृष्टः पुरुषविशेष ईश्वरः ॥

kleśakarmavipākāśayair aparāmṛṣṭaḥ puruṣaviśeṣa īśvaraḥ

kleśa: affliction, anguish, distress, pain
karman: action
vipāka: fruition
āśaya: deposit; the residue of previous actions, latent in the mind until surfacing in experience
aparāmṛṣṭa: untouched
puruṣa: consciousness, Self
viśeṣa: particularity, specificity, characteristic difference, aspect
īśvara: the Deity, God

As Patañjali continues in his methodical way, we understand that his reference to the Supreme Being is not such an unexpected thing after all. It is tied to the previous mention of latent impressions and their resurfacing.

The Supreme Being is, he explains, an "aspect of consciousness" free of conditioning. This all fits perfectly with what he has taught already. To gain freedom from the burden of accumulated mental impressions, he suggests intense contemplation of a higher aspect of consciousness, devoid of all the lingering impurity and limitation that *we* carry from the past.

The compound *puruṣaviṣeśa* is usually taken to mean a "distinct" or "special" *puruṣa.* This has given rise to a wealth of commentarial confusion in regard to defining God and soul. *Puruṣaviṣeśa* is better taken as a dependent (*tatpuruṣa*) compound meaning an "aspect (*viśeṣa*) of consciousness (*puruṣa*)." This reading makes better sense grammatically and philosophically. That aspect is consciousness as it is in itself—pure and unconditioned.

1.25 **There [in that divine reality, one finds], unsurpassed, the source of all knowledge.**

तत्र निरतिशयं सर्वज्ञबीजम् ॥

tatra niratiśayaṁ sarvajñabījam

tatra: there (in that state of unconditioned consciousness)
niratiśaya: unexcelled, unsurpassed
sārvajña: relating to or coming from that which is omniscient
bīja: seed, primary cause, source, origin, principle

Although we may have many different ideas of God, the highest reality is something we cannot even begin to imagine. The source of all knowledge is something *beyond* knowledge; it is the ultimate consciousness beyond the mind itself. It is the pure divine essence, which we attempt to describe as uncreated, eternal, never-changing awareness. That supreme consciousness is what we experience on reaching the goal of yoga, and that is what we recognize ourselves truly to be. As Patañjali pointed out in the third and fourth *sūtras* of this chapter, "To experience this is to abide in one's own essential nature. Otherwise one identifies with the mind's activities."

We have learned that we can use a number of different ways to still the mind. Some are purely psychological. This latest one is to meditate deeply on that higher aspect of consciousness that we sometimes call the Supreme Being. To do this is to bring a sacred dimension to our lives.

1.26 **Unbounded by time, that was also the guide of earlier seers.**

स पूर्वेषामपि गुरुः कालेनानवच्छेदात् ॥

sa pūrveṣām api guruḥ kālenānavacchedāt

sa: that (the Supreme Being)
pūrva: former, earlier, ancient, ancestor, forefather
api: also
guru: teacher, mentor, preceptor
kāla: time
anavaccheda: a not-particularizing, nonseparation

The divine reality always was, is, and will be available to every seeker. Just as the great sages and seers of times past found inspiration and guidance in something greater than themselves as individuals, so can we. As we keep to this practice, we find that the idea of divine presence grows into a sense of divine omnipresence. Everything becomes saturated in holiness, because there is no place where God is not.

1.27 **Its expression is the syllable OM.**

तस्य वाचकः प्रणवः ॥

tasya vācakaḥ praṇavaḥ

tasya: its, his
vācaka: expression, designation, symbol
praṇava: reverberation, the technical term for the syllable OM

If you want to get someone's attention, a good way is to say that person's name. If you want to make contact with the higher reality, the name to use is the sacred syllable OM. While most words are merely conventional symbols that vary from one language to another while the objects or ideas they represent stay the same, that is not the case with OM. This is no ordinary word. It has a deep connection with what it stands for. Its vibration embodies the divine presence, and its utterance is naturally filled with power. Patañjali tells us that OM is the *expression*—not just the symbol—of the Supreme Being.

OM is the seed of creation. Its four parts are the sounds *a, u, m,* and the reverberation that follows. Everything in creation has a beginning, a middle, and an end. The *a* relates to the beginning, the *u* to the continuing, and the *m* to the ending. Beyond that is eternity. The totality of OM signifies the world that comes into existence, remains for a while, and dissolves against the eternal backdrop of that uncreated and unchanging principle from which it arises and to which it returns.

But that is not all. Watch your mind. A thought arises, seemingly out of nowhere; it lingers for a while; then it fades away, seemingly into nowhere. All the while, *you are,* and the world exists in your awareness.

1.28 **[Constant] repetition of that [reveals] its meaning.**

तज्जपस्तदर्थभावनम् ॥

tajjapas tadarthabhāvanam

tad: its
japa: repetition (of a mantra), most often mentally as a spiritual practice to focus, calm, and clarify the mind
tad: its
artha: meaning
bhāvana: the act of producing or effecting in the mind, contemplation.

Why is the repetition of OM so effective? Because this syllable is not an ordinary word but rather an expression of divine energy. The OM you intone with the mouth is only its outward expression, involving the vibration of physical sound. The OM you repeat mentally is vibration of a subtler and higher order. The OM that you experience in deepest meditation takes you close to the divine source. Engaging the mind constantly with this sacred syllable will reveal its deepest meaning, and your awareness will be transformed.

This laconic *sūtra* reads, "Its constant repetition, contemplation of its meaning." Most commentators understand this in the sense that one *should* constantly repeat OM while meditating on its meaning. It can also be taken in the sense that the repetition of OM *leads* to the revelation of its meaning.

1.29 **Then one attains inner awareness, and obstacles do not arise.**

ततः प्रत्यक्चेतनाधिगमोऽप्यन्तरायाभावश्च ॥

tataḥ pratyakcetanādhigamo 'py antarāyābhāvaś ca

tatas: then, thereupon
pratyakcetanā: inward-mindedness
adhigama: attainment
api: also
antarāya: obstacle
abhāva: non-arising
ca: and

The mind begins to reflect the nature of the true Self dwelling deep within. Recall *sūtra* 1.24: "The Supreme Being is an aspect of consciousness untouched by [any] store of impressions that ripen into action and cause distress." This awareness of the divine presence expands the sense of self beyond the confines of the personality. At this stage you are not yet liberated, but you have begun to feel a greater sense of freedom from the demands and the reactions of the ego. Obstacles no longer arise to perturb you. What sorts of obstacles? Patañjali will name them in the next *sūtra*.

1.30 **Illness, apathy, doubt, negligence, laziness, dissipation, misapprehension, failure to reach concentration, and instability are the distractions of the mind; these are the obstacles.**

व्याधिस्त्यानसंशयप्रमादालस्याविरतिभ्रान्ति-
दर्शनालब्धभूमिकत्वानवस्थितत्वानि
चित्तविक्षेपास्तेऽन्तरायाः ॥

vyādistyānasaṁśayapramādālasyāviratibhrāntidarśanā-labdhabhūmikatvānavasthitatvāni cittavikṣepās te 'ntarāyāḥ

vyādi: disease, sickness, illness
styāna: idleness, apathy, languor
saṁśaya: doubt, indecision, hesitation
pramāda: heedlessness, carelessness, negligence
ālasya: laziness, sloth
avirati: dissipation
bhrāntidarśana: erroneous perception
alabdhabhūmikatva: unattained groundedness, failing to attain a certain state of concentration or awareness
anavasthitatva: instability
citta: mind
vikṣepa: distraction, scattering
te: they
antarāya: obstacles

The constant, mindful repetition of OM leads to an extraordinary serenity beyond life's usual disturbances, which Patañjali now enumerates.

A body that is physically ill calls attention to itself. The mind perceives pain or other unpleasant sensations and I identify with them. *My* back hurts, *I* am burning up with fever, *I* can't stop coughing. It's hard for the mind not to interact with the body and harder still to attempt any spiritual practice under those conditions.

Some obstacles are purely emotional. One of these is apathy. I just don't care.

Another obstacle is doubt. What if this yoga stuff doesn't really work? Am I just wasting my time and energy?

Then there's negligence. I figure yoga's the real thing, but there are other things I'd rather be doing.

Or laziness. I guess I just don't take yoga seriously enough. And sometimes I just don't feel like doing anything at all.

Or dissipation. Maybe I just want to do the things I know I shouldn't, like pursuing the wrong kinds of pleasure.

Or misapprehension. Maybe I'm not going about my meditation the right way. Maybe I didn't get the directions right, and that's why it's not working.

Or failure to reach concentration. Even if I *am* doing it right, I just can't seem to concentrate, no matter how hard I try.

And finally instability. On those rare occasions when the mind settles down, I can't keep it quiet for long, and then it's off and running again. How do you think *that* makes me feel?

1.31 **Accompanying [these] distractions [may be] misery, despondency, trembling, and gasping for breath.**

दुःखदौर्मनस्याङ्गमेजयत्वश्वासप्रश्वासा विक्षेपसहभुवः ॥

duḥkhadaurmanasyāṅgamejayatvaśvāsapraśvāsā vikṣepasahabhuvaḥ

duḥkha: unease, distress, pain, suffering
daurmanasya: despondency, dejection
aṅgamejayatva: trembling of the limbs or body
śvāsa: inhalation
praśvāsa: exhalation
vikṣepa: distraction
sahabhuva: occurring with, accompanying

How *do* I feel? Let's try to connect the symptoms listed here with the underlying physical and mental factors just named. Often the links are obvious, as in the case of a physical disease that produces bodily pain or trembling or irregular breathing. Negative thoughts can also produce misery, and this, if acute, can become anxiety or stress that also may manifest as tremors, gasping, or hyperventilation.

Sometimes the connections are less obvious and more complex. For instance, if you are sincere in your practice but fail to reach any level of concentration, feelings of failure can lead to frustration and depression. The combinations and connections of these negative factors are endless, but Patañjali's point is that as long as the mind is active and as long as negative factors remain, even buried as subconscious impressions, there is always the possibility that any of them can set off new chains of reactions. Because everything is interconnected in countless ways, all forms of negativity must be eradicated to prevent their consequent effects.

1.32 **These [distractions and their effects] can be avoided by bringing the mind repeatedly to a single focus.**

तत्प्रतिषेधार्थमेकतत्त्वाभ्यासः ॥

tatpratiṣedhārtham ekatattvābhyāsaḥ

tad: these
pratiṣedha: keeping back, warding off, prevention
artha: purpose
eka: one
tattva: object
abhyāsa: continuous practice, persistent endeavor, repeated exercise or discipline, diligence

There's nothing here that hasn't been said before. The point is, *you have to keep at it.* Still, Patañjali understands that most of us can't spend the whole of our lives sitting in meditation, nor would he advise it. His next eight *sūtras* will suggest ways to integrate our mindfulness into the broader panorama of living.

1.33 **Calmness and clarity of mind [result] from cultivating kindness toward the fortunate, compassion for the distressed, delight in the virtuous, and equanimity toward the unvirtuous.**

मैत्रीकरुणामुदितोपेक्षाणां सुखदुःखपुण्यापुण्य-
विषयाणां भावनातश्चित्तप्रसादनम् ॥

maitrīkaruṇāmuditopekṣāṇāṁ sukhaduḥkha-
puṇyāpuṇyaviṣayāṇāṁ bhāvanātaś cittaprasādanam

maitrī: friendliness, friendship, kindness
karuṇā: compassion
muditā: joy, gladness
upekṣā: equanimity
sukha: happiness, well-being
duḥkha: suffering, distress, unease
puṇya: virtuous, meritorious
āpuṇya: unvirtuous, unmeritorious

viṣaya: object
bhāvanātas: projecting, attitude
citta: mind
prasādana: calming, soothing, clearing

We are to cultivate positive attitudes internally and allow them to expand outward in relation to all other living beings.

Kindness should be felt and shown toward all. When Patañjali mentions kindness specifically toward the fortunate, he warns us gently to be alert for the possibility of jealousy or resentment that can arise from our own selfish feelings at the good fortune and happiness of others.

When he teaches compassion for those in distress, he likewise implies that when trying to help others, we should put aside our own feelings. "It's not about me" should always be the motto of one who serves lovingly and wisely. And the Sanskrit word for compassion does not mean just feeling pity toward someone; it means *doing something* to relieve another's suffering.

Many a spiritual seeker throughout the ages has been advised to seek the company of the holy. That is what "delight in the virtuous" means, and it too involves attitude. Another's moral excellence should never cause us to feel unworthy but should inspire us to become better ourselves.

How rare such inspiration is! Too often we encounter people who are the opposite of virtuous, and it is easy to take offense at how they think and act. Even if you dress up your reactions as "righteous indignation," what is the content of your mind? Those very faults and failings that you find so offensive in *them!* And as you think, so you become. The advice is to cultivate equanimity—dispassion—toward the unvirtuous. In other words, don't let them get to you.

Nurturing these four attitudes extends spiritual practice beyond the periods of sitting in meditation. All of our relations with other people in the course of a day can be forms of spiritual practice. This leads to inner peace and outward harmony, which are conducive to even higher states of awareness.

This *sūtra* shows that Patañjali was well aware of Buddhist practice and that the sources of the *Yogasūtra*'s teaching are broad-based. The four dispositions—*maitrī, karuṇā, muditā* and *upekṣā*—are what Buddhist teaching calls the four states of virtue (*brahmavihāras*) to be meditated upon and directed toward all beings.

1.34 **Or from [attention to] the outward flow and the pausing of the breath.**

प्रच्छर्दनविधारणाभ्यां वा प्राणस्य ॥

pracchardanavidhāraṇābhyāṁ vā prāṇasya

pracchardana: exhalation, a flowing forth
vidhāraṇa: checking, restraining, retention, stoppage
vā: or
prāṇa: breath

Another way to reach tranquility is by watching the natural flow of the breath. This is a time-honored technique of meditation and need not involve elaborate breathing exercises that pose risks to the nervous system and the mind.

When Patañjali speaks of exhalation, or the out-breath, he also implies inhalation, or the in-breath. You can't have one without the other. And at the junction of the two there occurs a momentary pause as the direction changes, so in fact breathing has three phases. By mindful attention to these three the flow becomes regular, and a state conducive to deeper contemplation results naturally and safely.

1.35 **Or [when] the outward flow of awareness toward an object arises, by observing that steadily.**

विषयवती वा प्रवृत्तिरुत्पन्ना मनसः स्थितिनिबन्धनी ॥

viṣayavatī vā pravṛttir utpannā manasaḥ sthitinibandhanī

viṣayavatī: having an object
vā: or

pravṛtti: outward flow of awareness
utpanna: arisen, come forth, appeared, produced
manas: the function of mind that receives and processes sensory information
sthiti: steadiness
nibandhanin: holding

Like the breath, which has an inward and an outward flow, the mind also "flows" outward toward the objects of perception and inward toward self-awareness.

If you focus intensely on the perception of an object, your perceptivity regarding that object will grow ever keener. You will begin to feel a connection with it, and what started as an outward flow of consciousness will become internalized. Your knowledge of that object becomes uniquely your own. This is true of any interest that you pursue. The more you apply yourself and the deeper your understanding grows, the more you see beyond the outward appearance. Your understanding penetrates to subtler levels.

This is also true of the spiritual pursuit. Suppose that you focus intently on a sacred image or a passage from a sacred text. Your knowledge of it begins with the initial impression of something external but becomes internalized, and it is there that deepening insight dawns.

1.36 **Or [by focusing on a state] free from anguish and filled with the light of intelligence.**

विशोका वा ज्योतिष्मती ॥

viśokā vā jyotiṣmatī

viśoka: free of sorrow, affliction, anguish, pain, trouble, grief
vā: or
jyotiṣmatī: brilliant; filled with the divine light of intelligence, freedom, and joy

Some of the classic texts on yoga advise us to retire to a solitary place when we meditate. The best solitary place is within, in the "cave" of the heart, meaning the center of our own awareness. Withdrawn from external events and sensory stimuli, we can try to turn our awareness back on itself. If we succeed, we find that by nature it is free of disturbances of any kind and self-luminous. This gives us an intimation of true freedom and joy.

1.37 **Or by [directing] the mind [toward] an object that does not arouse passion.**

वीतरागविषयं वा चित्तम् ॥

vītarāgaviṣayaṁ vā cittam

vītarāga: free from attraction, desire, attachment, or passion
viṣaya: object
vā: or
citta: mind; one's individual field of consciousness

In trying to make the mind one-pointed, focus your attention on something that does not arouse any reaction. Three *sūtras* earlier Patañjali suggested that we focus on an object that engages our rapt attention. Now he suggests focusing on something that we regard with complete neutrality. This is another step forward in managing the mind.

Vyāsa and company advise us to meditate on the figures of the great saints and sages who have overcome attachment or passion. The Sanskrit can just as readily be understood, and to better avail perhaps, as instruction to meditate on *objects* that do not incite reactions rather than on *people* who have overcome them.

1.38 **Or by resting on knowledge [had] in dream or sleep.**

स्वप्ननिद्राज्ञानालम्बनं वा ॥

svapnanidrājñānālambanaṁ vā

svapna: dream

nidrā: deep sleep
jñāna: knowledge
ālambana: depending on, resting upon
vā: or

We have to take into account that although more than two-thirds of human life is spent in the waking state, a third or so is divided between dreaming and deep sleep. There is obviously mental activity in dreaming, and in dreamless sleep also, as *sūtra* 1.10 explained. Beyond these three states of ordinary consciousness—and pervading them—is a state of pure awareness known simply as "the fourth."

In the waking state the mind perceives other people, objects, circumstances, and events, and interacts with them through the physical body. In the dream state, independent of the world outside, the mind perceives and interacts with a world that it generates internally by its own power of ideation. The waking state is one of shared experiences. We all see the same world, filled with people, other living creatures, and material objects, even though we each experience them in our own unique way. In dreaming, a person may see the same things as when awake, because a dream consists of whatever was previously impressed on the mind in the waking state. But now that appears to the dreamer alone and in a purely mental form. A dream is not a shared experience.

In dreamless sleep there is no longer an awareness of objects as such. On waking, a person might say, "I knew nothing." The pronoun *I* affirms that the individual was present in the state of deep sleep. The verb *knew* affirms that some sort of mental activity was taking place. *Nothing* is the object, expressed in negative terms, but an object nevertheless. Recall Patañjali's definition in *sūtra* 1.10: "Sleep is mental activity based on the awareness of nothingness."

The effects of a dream can persist even after we've awakened. A nightmare can leave us feeling unsettled even though we dismiss it as "just a bad dream." But a dream with a spiritual content can have a positive and long-lasting effect.

After dreamless sleep we awaken refreshed and renewed. The positive effects of a holy dream and the sense of deep peace that results from dreamless sleep can be used as the focus of meditation, acknowledging and integrating the non-waking periods into our spiritual practice.

1.39 **Indeed, by meditating however one wishes.**

यथाभिमतध्यानाद्वा ॥

yathābhimatadhyānād vā

yathā: as, according to
abhimata: longed for, wished, desired, loved, dear
dhyāna: meditation
vā: or, just, even, indeed

Through the inner instrument that is the mind, we experience everything in our lives. Although of a subtler nature than the physical organs, like them the mind has its specific tasks. In principle, this instrument itself is probably the same for everyone, just like the heart, which circulates the blood, or the lungs, which move the air in and out.

However, while the heartbeat and the breath function more or less the same for everyone, the experiences of the mind and its accrued impressions are infinitely varied.

Patañjali has emphasized the spiritual goal of stilling the mind's activity through the principle of one-pointed attention and has suggested a variety of ways to bring this about. They are all proven methods. Now, in view of the endless possibilities open to each of us, he acknowledges that there are untold other ways to bring the mind to a state of focused serenity, owing to the uniqueness of each human personality. Whatever works, go for it—that's the message.

1.40 **Mastery [in meditation encompasses everything] from the infinitesimal to the most immense.**

परमाणुपरममहत्त्वान्तोऽस्य वशीकारः ॥

paramāṇuparamamahattvānto 'sya vaśīkāraḥ

parama: to the greatest degree
aṇu: minute (as an atom)
parama: most, greatest
mahattva: magnitude
anta: end
asya: of it (meditation)
vaśīkāra: mastery

Summing up the discussion begun in *sūtra* 1.32, Patañjali reminds us that whatever the object of concentration, our attention must be total. The object of choice may the subtlest and finest thing imaginable, no larger than an atom; or it may be the vastness of the clear and cloudless sky, a visible symbol of infinity. Through unwavering attention stillness is reached.

1.41 **When mental activity lessens, [the mind becomes] like a transparent crystal [that reflects the color of any object nearby]. The [mind's] coloring by whatever comes before it—[be that the idea of] the knower, the knowing, or the known—is [called] convergence.**

क्षीणवृत्तेरभिजातस्येव मणेर्ग्रहीतृग्रहणग्राह्येषु
तत्स्थतदञ्जनता समापत्तिः ॥

kṣīṇavṛtter abhijātasyeva maṇer grahītṛgrahaṇagrāhyeṣu
tatsthatadañjanatā samāpattiḥ

kṣīṇa: vitiated, weakened, diminished, fading away
vṛtti: mental activity, "thought-wave"
abhijāta: transparent
iva: like
maṇi: jewel, gem, crystal
grahītṛ: grasper, knower
grahaṇa: grasping, the process of knowing
grāhya: that which is to be grasped, the known object
tad: that

stha: being in or on, situated
tad: that
añjanatā: coloration
samāpatti: a coming together, convergence, an assuming of a particular state or condition (with something else)

Here Patañjali begins a more technical and challenging look at the mind and how it works. He gives the classic illustration of a crystal. Having no color of its own but only pure clarity, it appears to take on the color of anything nearby.

In any ordinary experience, in any act of knowledge, there is a knower, something known, and the knowing that relates them. Any one of these three aspects of mental activity can become the focus of meditation: the self as knower, any object of choice, even the act of knowing. Once concentrated, the mind becomes sufficiently clarified, and it will be "colored" only by whatever is immediately present. This state is called convergence, because it is a genuine coming together of the mind and the focus of thought.

1.42 **There, when intermixed with concepts of word, meaning, and understanding, convergence is [said to be] accompanied by thought.**

तत्र शब्दार्थज्ञानविकल्पैः संकीर्णा सवितर्का समापत्तिः ॥

tatra śabdārthajñānavikalpaiḥ saṁkīrṇā savitarkā samāpattiḥ

tatra: there (in convergence)
śabda: sound, word, speech, language
artha: meaning, intent, purpose
jñāna: knowledge, knowing
vikalpa: concept
saṁkīrṇa: interspersed, mixed into
savitarka: accompanied by reason or thought, rational, deliberative, cogitative
samāpatti: coming together, convergence

We've reached a degree of intense concentration on a physical object, let's say an apple. What is present to the mind? First the image of the apple—its form and color. Next comes the idea of the word *apple,* which also suggests further ideas of what we think an apple is—a fragrant, tasty, health-giving fruit that we may or may not like. It turns out that our attention is not focused just on the apple but on an assortment of accompanying factors. The mind is occupied not only with the physical object, but also with the word that represents it, along with a lot of information about apples imprinted from our previous experiences.

It doesn't matter what the object is; at this level of concentration, all those associated factors are present. Patañjali's name for this state of mind is "convergence accompanied by thought." Because it is an experience of the object mixed together with words and ideas, it is not completely focused.

1.43 **When [the mind is] cleared of memory, seemingly empty of any character of its own and shining forth in identification with the object alone, convergence [is said to be] thought-free.**

स्मृतिपरिशुद्धौ स्वरूपशून्येवार्थमात्रनिर्भासा

निर्वितर्का ॥

smṛtipariśuddhau svarūpaśūnyevārthamātranirbhāsā nirvitarkā

smṛti: memory
pariśuddhi: purification, cleaning, becoming cleared of
svarūpa: own form, nature, character, condition
śūnya: void, empty
iva: like, as if
arthamātra: being only the matter itself, identification
nirbhāsa: shining forth
nirvitarka: not involving thinking or reasoning, knowing or learning of something without the conscious use of deliberation, instantaneously apprehended, intuitive

We can reach a still deeper state of attentiveness in which the mind becomes so focused on the object alone that all associated words, ideas, memories, and impressions drop away, *along with the meditator's own sense of personality.* This deeper, reaction-free state of the mind's coming together with a material object is called "thought-free convergence." Here the cognitive processes that ordinarily accompany the object have all but ceased.

1.44 **In the same way, [convergence] in regard to subtle objects is [described as] with reflection and free of reflection.**

एतयैव सविचारा निर्विचारा च सूक्ष्मविषया व्याख्याता ॥

etayaiva savicārā nirvicārā ca sūkṣmaviṣayā vyākhyātā

etayā: by this
eva: thus
savicāra: with pondering, deliberation, consideration, or reflection
nirvicāra: without pondering, deliberation, consideration, or reflection
ca: and
sūkṣma: subtle
viṣaya: object
vyākhyāta: named, called, explained, described

The two previous *sūtras* dealt with concentration on a physical object—something with shape, volume, color, and other characteristics knowable to the senses. It is unlikely that anyone would choose to meditate on our apple for spiritual inspiration, and the "object" of choice more likely would be the envisioned form of a deity or sacred symbol or a concept. Granted, our first experience of such an object may come through sense perception. We may see an image in a shrine or hear the syllable OM or hear a spiritual principle explained.

But then we take it to another level. The focus of our concentration is no longer something seen with the eyes or heard with the ears but ideated within. It may not even be an iconographic form but an abstraction, a concept of the Divine as a formless principle, an essence beyond all appearance. As with the physical object, initial focus on the subtle object will be accompanied by the words that represent it and by the thoughts and feelings that arise in connection with it. Patañjali calls this level of concentration "convergence with reflection." It is different from "convergence accompanied by thought" only in having a nonphysical or subtle object as its focus.

In this higher state, awareness no longer just adheres to the subtle object of meditation but begins to penetrate it. Once we become so focused that the verbal symbols and descriptive concepts and associations drop away from our contemplation, we reach the state of "convergence free of reflection," where penetrating insight into the object's true nature occurs.

1.45 **Furthermore, subtle objectivity reaches its end in the undifferentiated.**

सूक्ष्मविषयत्वं चालिङ्गपर्यवसानम् ॥

sūkṣmaviṣayatvaṁ cāliṅgaparyavasānam

sūkṣma: subtle
viṣayatva: objectivity
ca: and, also, moreover
aliṅga: undifferentiated, without any distinguishing qualities
paryavasāna: end, termination, conclusion

Having advanced to the point where almost all mental activity has stopped, we have left behind our perception of material objects and the thoughts that arise in connection with them. We have gone beyond the conception of abstract principles and any associated ideas. We are about to come face to face with the principle of objectivity itself out of which the cosmos evolves. This state of awareness is not yet liberation, because there remains an interaction between knower and knowable, however rarefied that may be.

1.46 **Those [four kinds of convergence] are [aspects of] meditative union with seed.**

ता एव सबीजः समाधिः ॥

tā eva sabījaḥ samādhiḥ

tā: those
eva: indeed, surely
sabīja: with seed, having the potentiality to manifest
samādhi: meditative union, unitary consciousness

Although Patañjali has described and named four different levels of intensive meditation, it would be a mistake to think that we jump from box to box or climb from one rung of the ladder to the next. They are merely points along a continuum as our consciousness flows back toward the heart of awareness. The degree of awareness proceeds from initial focus or one-pointedness, deepening to convergence, and finally reaching union. It's all a matter of degree.

When sufficiently intensified and prolonged, the four kinds of convergence just described reach the point of absorption. Patañjali can now call them "union with seed." By this he means that even they are not the highest experience of yoga. We still return to ordinary awareness and are liable to get as caught up in the affairs of daily living as before because of latent impressions just waiting to be reactivated. Until the potential for future involvement is gone, we are not free.

1.47 **In the clarity of [the fourth kind of convergence], free of reflection, the serene radiance of the higher Self [shines forth].**

निर्विचारवैशारद्येऽध्यात्मप्रसादः ॥

nirvicāravaiśāradye 'dhyātmaprasādaḥ

nirvicāra: without deliberation, intuitive
vaiśāradya: lucidity, clearness of intellect, infallibility, experience, wisdom
adhyātman: the supreme spirit, one's own Self
prasāda: clarity, brightness, purity, calmness, serenity

When consciousness is aware only of its nearly content-free state, when there is little else to claim attention, when even the *possibility* of an object dissolves away, what is left? Only the intuitive clarity of consciousness itself, which Patañjali calls "the serene radiance of the higher Self."

1.48 **The insight there is self-evident truth.**

ऋतम्भरा तत्र प्रज्ञा ॥

ṛtambharā tatra prajñā

ṛta: proper order, divine law, truth, righteousness
bharā: bearing
tatra: there, in that
prajñā: wisdom, intuitive insight
(ṛtaṁbharā prajñā: wisdom or knowledge that contains the truth in itself)

There is nothing more to say. There is no longer a thinking mind or its thoughts or any need for explanation. The direct experience of one's true being simply *is,* inexpressibly so.

1.49 **[This insight] belongs to a domain different from that of knowledge gained through learning and inference, because [the latter is] driven by distinction.**

श्रुतानुमानप्रज्ञाभ्यामन्यविषया विशेषार्थत्वात् ॥

śrutānumānaprajñābhyām anyaviṣayā viśeṣārthatvāt

śruta: learning, teaching, instruction
anumāna: inference, consideration, reflection

prajñā: intuitive insight
anya: other, different from
viṣaya: sphere, domain
viśeṣa: distinction, difference, characteristic difference
arthatva: intentionality, motivation

Beyond any relative knowledge dependent on the limitations of thought or language, the highest insight is direct experience of the true Self—unitary consciousness, self-evident and self-luminous.

1.50 **The impression born from [this insight] prevents any further impressions [from forming].**

तज्जः संस्कारोऽन्यसंस्कारप्रतिबन्धी ॥

tajjaḥ saṁskāro 'nyasaṁskārapratibandhī

tad: that
ja: born, produced, belonging to, connected with, peculiar to
saṁskāra: latent impression
anya: other
saṁskāra: latent impression
pratibandhin: obstructing, impeding

We learn here how, finally, complete stillness—the goal of yoga—is attained. The experience of the real Self is so overwhelming that nothing else could ever again leave its mark on our awareness. The myriad impressions we have been accumulating, moment by moment from lifetime to lifetime, dissolve away in the ineffable light of Self-recognition.

1.51 **By stilling even this [final impression], by stilling everything, [one reaches] the seedless [state of] transcendental consciousness.**

तस्यापि निरोधे सर्वनिरोधान्निर्बीजः समाधिः ॥

tasyāpi nirodhe sarvanirodhān nirbījaḥ samādhiḥ

tasya: of this (obstruction)
api: also
nirodha: restraint, check, control
sarva: all
nirodha: restraint, check, control
nirbīja: without seed; beyond the potentiality to manifest
samādhi: meditative union, unitary consciousness

Yoga, which began as a practice, we now know as the goal. Patañjali describes this supreme awareness as "without seed," because never again will the soul be bound. One who is thus illumined is said to be free even in this life. Or perhaps, in truth, the soul was never bound.

The Sāṁkhya term for liberation is *kaivalya,* understood as "perfect isolation," meaning the complete disengagement or liberation of consciousness (*puruṣa*) from matter (*prakṛti*). In contrast, nondualistic schools such as Advaita Vedānta understand the word *kaivalya* to mean "absolute Oneness," signifying liberation through the attainment of unitary consciousness—Brahman—recognized as the sole and infinite reality.

The classical commentators expounded a variety of opinions on the nature of liberation. Two of their views warrant mention here.

Vyāsa, conforming to the Sāṁkhya position, declared that once the mind has been utterly stilled through yogic practice and dissolved along with its potentialities into the undifferentiated matrix (*prakṛti*), then *puruṣa* alone remains in its own true being, released (*mukta*) and absolutely free.

Writing a thousand years later, Vijñānabhikṣu contended from the Vedāntic point of view that that *puruṣa* has always been free. His opinion reflects that of Gauḍapāda, a near contemporary of Vyāsa's and the founder of the Advaita Vedānta school. Gauḍapāda, who spoke from the loftiness of nondual realization, summarized his doctrine of nonorigination in the *Māṇḍūkyakārikā* (2.32):

> There is neither dissolution nor origination; there are none bound and none striving, none longing for liberation, and none liberated. This is the absolute truth.

CHAPTER 2

2.1 **Ardent discipline, study, and mindfulness of the sacred [make up] the yoga of action.**

तपःस्वाध्यायेश्वरप्रणिधानानि क्रियायोगः ॥

tapaḥsvādhyāyeśvarapraṇidhānāni kriyāyogaḥ

tapas: ardent discipline, heat, religious austerity
svādhyāya: study (of sacred teaching)
īśvarapraṇidhāna: cultivation of a fixed and respectful mindfulness of the Divine (*see* 1.23)
kriyā: action
yoga: the act of joining, union, means, way, manner, method, application or concentration of thought

In the first chapter Patañjali described the mind, how it works, and how we can manage it for our own benefit. He taught that yoga is the stilling of mental activity and that it is both the way to reach the goal and the goal itself.

He described two kinds of awareness: the ordinary awareness of daily living and the higher awareness of the true Self, beyond the limitations of time and space and cause and effect. In ordinary awareness each of us has the sense that I am an individual, identified with a human body and personality. In this world of "I and other" everything revolves around me. I see the world from my own unique and central vantage point. I know both happiness and misery. In contrast, the second kind of awareness is the enlightenment of Self-knowledge, in which I abide in the indescribable peace, joy, and freedom of my true being.

Patañjali outlined how the mind keeps us bound to mere human existence and how it can be redirected toward liberation. He described progressive states of higher and higher consciousness along the way and emphasized that yoga involves constant, repeated endeavor.

Now he starts the second chapter by telling us how to begin our practice, laying out a plan that he calls the "yoga of action." This yoga of action involves how we behave and think and feel. In regard to our behavior, it calls for ardent discipline—a sincere, enthusiastic resolve to get the upper hand over our natural cravings and impulses. As for thinking, the study of sacred teachings awakens us to the wisdom and spiritual vision of great souls who have reached enlightenment before us. As for feeling, like them we must foster a personal awareness of what we deem sacred and make it a constant presence in our lives. Later we shall gain a deeper understanding of each of these three practices.

Commentators do not agree on what Patañjali meant by the yoga of action (*kriyāyoga*). Vyāsa saw it as the beginning steps for those who were not sufficiently advanced to follow the teachings already set forth in the first chapter. Vācaspati Miśra held that *kriyā yoga* is a preliminary stage designed to purify and prepare the normally outgoing mind for the practice of repeated endeavor (*abhyās*a) and dispassion (*vairāgya*) that lead to the higher states of consciousness.

Georg Feuerstein (in *The Yoga-Sūtra of Patañjali,* pp. 59–60) sees two distinct systems of yoga. The first, he contends, is Patañjali's own *kriyāyoga,* and the second (from *sūtra* 2.28 onward) is the eight-limbed (*aṣṭāṇga*) yoga, which he believes Patañjali took from another source. Bryant (pp. xxxvi–xxxvii) finds it "very plausible" that Patañjali drew upon and merged two different yogic traditions.

In support of Vyāsa's view of *kriyāyoga* as a preliminary practice, it is noteworthy that its three elements—*tapas, svādhyāya,* and *īśvara-praṇidhāna*—are also elements of *aṣṭāṅga yoga*'s second limb, which is a preparatory phase of cultivating positive dispositions.

2.2 **[The yoga of action] is aimed at weakening [the mind's] distress and bringing about meditative union.**

समाधिभावनार्थः क्लेशतनूकरणार्थश्च ॥

samādhibhāvanārthaḥ kleśatanūkaraṇārthaś ca

samādhi: meditative union, unitary consciousness
bhāvana: bringing about, cultivating
artha: purpose
kleśa: affliction, anguish, distress, pain
tanū: attenuated, weak
karaṇa: making
ārtha: purpose
ca: and

Whatever we do, it's normal to seek the satisfaction of positive results. Should the practice of yoga be any different? When we step back from our usual reactivity and begin to recognize the distressing factors of life for what they really are, we begin to feel a greater sense of peace. We also learn how to become more and more focused in meditation and to aspire to meditative union. Enlightenment or liberation will not happen all at once, because there is much to be changed in our habits of acting and thinking and feeling, but continued practice of the yoga of action will slowly but surely make a difference.

2.3 **The [causes of] distress are ignorance, ego, attraction, aversion, and the force of habit.**

अविद्यास्मितारागद्वेषाभिनिवेशाः क्लेशाः ॥

avidyāsmitārāgadveṣābhiniveśāḥ kleśāḥ

avidyā: ignorance, nescience, unknowing
asmitā: "I-am-ness," egoity, ego
rāga: attraction, attachment
dveṣa: aversion
abhiniveśa: tenacity, adherence, holding on (to the familiar), the force of habit
kleśa: affliction, anguish, distress, pain

Patañjali loses no time in getting to the heart of the human condition. He sums it up in five words that mean ignorance of our true being, the sense of individuality, attraction, aversion, and clinging to what we are used to. If we seek the causes of any discomfort or unease that life can bring, we need look no further than these five.

2.4 **Ignorance is the ground of the others, [which may appear as] dormant, weak, intermittent, or fully active.**

अविद्या क्षेत्रमुत्तरेषां प्रसुप्ततनुविच्छिन्नोदाराणाम् ॥

avidyā kṣetram uttareṣāṁ prasuptatanuvicchinodārāṇām

avidyā: ignorance, nescience, unknowing, the ignorance of one's true being
kṣetra: field (a metaphor for the individual's field of awareness)
uttara: other
prasupta: dormant, at rest in the subconscious mind
tanu: attentuated, weak
vicchinna: intermittent, interrupted, as when attention shifts from one thing to another
udāra: fully active, manifest

Before we look individually at the causes of unease, Patañjali wants us to understand two things. The first of the five causes gives rise to the other four; ignorance of our essential nature is the fertile ground in which the others take root and thrive. The second point is that those four factors operate in different ways and in varying degrees while the underlying ignorance on which they rest is constant.

The deeply rooted patterns of ego, attraction, aversion, and clinging to the familiar may not always be apparent. They may retreat to just below the surface of our awareness, ever ready to rise up and cause trouble. When they rise up, their expression may be weak or half-hearted. Even if more forceful, any one of them can be interrupted by the flaring up of one of the others. This "on again, off again" state is a sign of how volatile the mind is, how subject to changing moods. Should one of these pain-bearing impulses become fully aroused, it will eclipse all the others for a time.

2.5 **Ignorance is seeing the eternal, pure, joyful Self as the impermanent, impure, distressing non-self.**

अनित्याशुचिदुःखानात्मसु नित्यशुचिसुखात्म-
ख्यातिरविद्या ॥

anityāśuciduḥkhānātmasu nityaśucisukhātmakhyātir avidyā

anitya: noneternal, impermanent, temporal, transient, ephemeral
aśuci: impure
duḥkha: unpleasant, distressing
anātman: non-self
nitya: eternal, unchanging
śuci: pure
sukha: pleasant, giving comfort or ease
ātman: Self
khyāti: seeing, knowing, notion, perception
avidyā: ignorance, nescience, unknowing

Ignorance is nonawareness, you might say forgetfulness, of our essential being, of who and what we truly are. It is not a total absence of awareness, for if that were so, we would have no experience even of our own existence. By *ignorance* Patañjali simply means not getting it right. Being unaware of our true nature leaves us wide open to creating our own mistaken ideas of who we are.

Patañjali makes his point by evoking some pairs of opposites. We are unaware that our true nature is eternal. Instead we see ourselves (and everything else) as impermanent, and that can be a source of distress. We want some things to last forever. We are unaware that our true being is the absolute purity of consciousness itself. Instead we allow our awareness to be colored by anything and everything that comes before it, and we lose sight of our inherent perfection. The word *impure* does not necessarily mean dirty or defiled; it simply means limited by whatever we see as different or apart from ourselves. Our original nature is unalloyed joy, identical with the freedom of wholeness.

Long before Patañjali's time the Chāndogyopaniṣad (7.23.1–24.1) offered these observations:

> The Infinite alone is happiness; there is no happiness in the finite. The Infinite indeed is happiness, but one must desire to understand the Infinite. ... Where one sees nothing else, hears nothing else, discerns nothing else, that is the Infinite. But where one sees something else, hears something else, discerns something else, that is the finite. Truly, what is infinite is immortal, but what is finite is mortal.

2.6 **Ego [is just] identifying the nature of the perceiver with the nature of the perception.**

दृग्दर्शनशक्त्योरेकात्मतेवास्मिता ॥

dṛgdarśanaśaktyor ekātmatevāsmitā

dṛk: seer, perceiver (the subjective aspect of consciousness)
darśana: seeing, perception
śakti: power, energy, ability, capability
ekātmatā: identity ("one-self-ness")
iva: as if, as it were, just
asmitā: ego, egoity, "I-am-ness"

Early in the first chapter, in *sūtra* 1.3, Patañjali taught that to experience enlightenment is to abide in our own essential nature. Otherwise we identify with whatever comes before the mind. This identification is the work of the ego, which is a part of the mind, and the mind is only an instrument of knowing. Consciousness itself, and not the mind, is the true knower. We've just forgotten this. Instead the ego claims the ability to perceive and to know as its own. We reinforce this idea every time we say, "I know."

The power of perceiving or seeing or knowing that the ego-self claims to possesses is different from the higher Self-awareness, because it involves *something other than the Self.* The previous *sūtra* said as much when it defined ignorance as "seeing the eternal, pure, joyful Self as the impermanent, impure, distressing non-self." One who is enlightened experiences the self-aware Self. "Otherwise," as Patañjali says in *sūtra* 1.4, "one identifies with the mind's activities." Such an experience of who I am brings together many things that have come before the mind. From them I have fashioned my own sense of individuality. This personality, with all its history, is a burden of misidentification with body, mind, perceptions, stored impressions, likes, dislikes, opinions, expectations, and consequences from which I am never free.

Let's take it a step further. This mistaken sense of self, based on identifying with things and qualities of an objective nature, is itself objectified. What do I think of *myself?* What do others think of *me?* I, the apparent subject, become an object to be judged. This mixture of Self and not-self becomes a source of doubt, distress, unhappiness, and misery.

Why? Because this mistaken sense of identity has a shaky foundation. What is objective comes and goes. How I feel about myself changes from moment to moment. Favorable conditions bring confidence, joy, or a feeling of self-worth; but something as slight as an unkind word can banish well-being in an instant, triggering feelings of doubt, inadequacy, anger, or fear. Which self is the real me? The one now or the one a moment ago?

2.7 **Attraction results from what is pleasant.**

सुखानुशयी रागः ॥

sukhānuśayī rāgaḥ

sukha: pleasant, happy
anuśayin: following upon, connected with as a consequence
rāga: attraction, attachment

From the underlying forgetfulness of who I truly am develops the sense of who I think I am. From that ego-generated self springs a sense of what attracts me and what I choose to like, impressed on the mind in pleasant ways. Is this all fine and good? No, because it is also what I may be driven to pursue. The ego-self is reactive to circumstances, in contrast to the supreme Self, which is the ever-free witness.

2.8 **Aversion results from what is unpleasant.**

दुःखानुशायी द्वेषः ॥

duḥkhānuśayī dveṣaḥ

duḥkha: unpleasant, distressing
anuśayin: following upon, connected with as a consequence
dveṣa: aversion

Here we have the other side of the coin. What pleases me, I wish to experience again and again. What brings unpleasantness, I wish to avoid. Either way, I am not in charge. I am reactive. In order to be free of conditioning, I must learn to overcome the pull and push of attraction and aversion alike. I must refrain from chasing after that which I believe will make me happy, as much as I must refrain from running away from that which I think will bring misery. Patañjali has already shown the way. It is the cultivation of dispassion.

2.9 **The force of habit is a self-perpetuating tendency rooted even in the wise.**

स्वरसवाही विदुषोऽपि तथा रूढोऽभिनिवेशः ॥

svarasavāhī viduṣo 'pi tathā rūḍho 'bhiniveśaḥ

svarasavāhin: carrying along its own inclination, self-perpetuating
vidvāṁs: wise one, knowing one, sage
api: even
tathā: thus
rūḍha: rooted, established
abhiniveśa: tenacity, adherence, the force of habit (often taken as the will to live, the clinging to life)

The cultivation of dispassion faces an obstacle—the force of habit. Think of this fifth cause of affliction and how it relates to the other four. The process begins with the forgetfulness of our original spiritual perfection. With that ignorance in place, the sense arises that I am an individual. As such I interact with my surroundings, finding some things attractive and others not, some things promising satisfaction and others threatening discomfort. I become reactive and form patterns in my attitudes and behavior. Whatever comes before the mind leaves its mark in the form of a subconscious impression, and with repetition our positive or negative responses—our patterns of attitude and behavior—become deeply ingrained. Such is the force of habit.

Now it's not simply that we react positively to anything good and negatively to anything bad. What one person sees as good may appear as bad to someone else. What one person seeks out as desirable, another may want to shun. There is no impartial measure of the reasons for attraction and aversion. Even within a single person it's not a simple matter of black and white. What may attract me now may repel me later, depending on the time and circumstances.

And there's more. The force of habit is about sticking with what is familiar and being comfortable, to a degree, even with that which is not exactly comforting or which we know is not in our best interest. Why? Our habituality is empowered by fear of change, fear of the unfamiliar, and a desire for the status quo. As the five causes of affliction unfold, with the force of habit we are stuck at the end of the line in the condition called bondage.

Vyāsa takes the word *abhiniveśa* to mean a "clinging to life," owing to painful, subconscious impressions of past death experiences. Monier-Williams's dictionary gives no such definition. There the meanings include "application, intentness, determination, tenacity, or adherence." Apte's dictionary concurs but adds that in Yoga philosophy *abhiniveśa* refers to a kind of ignorance causing an instinctive clinging to worldly enjoyments and the fear of their curtailment by death. This specialized definition may be Vyāsa's own creation. His short-sighted view deprives us of a fuller, more useful understanding of *abhiniveśa* in terms of how we *live.* Even though the instinctive desire for self-preservation is universal, we are not always preoccupied with thoughts of our own mortality, but we almost always are the victims of our own self-created habits.

2.10 **These [five causes of distress], which are subtle, can be overcome by reversing the flow of consciousness.**

ते प्रतिप्रसवहेयाः सूक्ष्माः ॥

te pratiprasavaheyāḥ sūkṣmāḥ

te: they, these
pratiprasava: counter-flow, return to an original state (of pure, unconditioned consciousness)
heya: to abandoned, rejected, gotten rid of
sūkṣma: subtle

We know the underlying causes of human distress by their effects. The first of them, ignorance of our true being, gives rise to the other four. Ignorance is the fertile ground from which the others spring up, and those are at any time either dormant, weak, off-and-on, or fully active, producing the ever-changing and wide-ranging variety of human experience. To whichever degree they become evident (or even rest inactive) these pain-bearing principles can and must be overcome.

If we wish to clear a field, we have to pull out every last plant by its roots. In the same way, we can get rid of these causes of affliction only by uprooting them. How? By a "counter-flow" of consciousness—that is, by ceasing to direct mental activity outward into the world and redirecting it back to the original consciousness from which it springs.

The word *vṛtti* refers to mental activity within the individual's own field of awareness (*citta*). Its outward flow (*pravṛtti*) produces awareness of an exterior world with which we interact. The inward flow (*nivṛtti*) takes us back to the source, and that source is the supreme Self, the ultimate seer. When that pure consciousness-as-subject appears to flow outward through the capacity of seeing (which means the capacities of all five senses), it experiences an association of subject and object, and then, through the function of the ego, the mistaken sense of a separate, personal identity results. That conditioned sense of personal identity becomes subject to all manner of experiences—pleasant, painful, and everything in between. To go beyond this limitation, we need to relinquish all claim to those five *kleśas*—the principles of ignorance of our true being, ego, attraction, aversion, and habituality. We need to reverse the outward flow of consciousness toward the finite and imperfect and allow our awareness to flow back toward the blissful stillness and wholeness of its original, content-free perfection.

2.11 **The [mind's] changing states can be nullified through meditation.**

ध्यानहेयास्तद्वृत्तयः ॥

dhyānaheyās tadvṛttayaḥ

dhyāna: meditation
heya: to be left, quitted, abandoned, rejected, avoided
tad: that, of these
vṛtti: activity, function, occupation with, mode of conduct

The eight-limbed yoga which Patañjali will explain systematically beginning with *sūtra* 2.28 is a gradual process of turning inward, beginning with our relationship with the surrounding world, then refining our inner dispositions and moving step by step back to our true, original nature.

Meditation is the seventh of the eight steps. For now,

Patañjali tells us only that it is the way to reverse the flow of consciousness and to rid ourselves of the causes of distress.

2.12 **The cumulative results of [past] actions, to be experienced now or in the future, are rooted in the [five] causes of distress.**

क्लेशमूलः कर्माशयो दृष्टादृष्टजन्मवेदनीयः ॥

kleśamūlaḥ karmāśayo dṛṣṭādṛṣṭajanmavedanīyaḥ

kleśa: affliction, anguish, distress, pain
mūla: root, origin
karman: action
āśaya: the deposit of the fruits of previous actions, lying latent in the mind until they ripen into the individual's experience
dṛṣṭa: seen, visible, experienced, present
adṛṣṭa: unseen, unforeseen, future
janman: birth, coming into existence, production
vedanīya: to be experienced

As long as we fail to uproot the five causes of the human condition, they continue to produce their present and future effects in ways we can see and in ways unforeseen.

This *sūtra* reaffirms a principle of causality at work in our lives, expressed in Indian philosophies as karma. Whatever our actions may be, whether in thought, word, or deed, they bear consequences. Those actions themselves are rooted in the five factors of ignorance, ego, attraction, aversion, and habit. What we are now is the result of what we have done in the past, and what we *do* now is for the most part the product of what we *are* now. That will in turn determine the future. That's why it is so hard to break free.

2.13 **As long as a root cause exists, it will ripen into [the conditions of] birth, life, and experience.**

सति मूले तद्विपाको जात्यायुर्भोगाः ॥

sati mūle tadvipāko jātyāyurbhogāḥ

sati: being
mūla: root
tad: that, it
vipāka: ripening, maturation. fruition
jāti: birth
āyus: lifetime, span of life
bhoga: experience

The conditions into which we are born, our innate personal qualities, as well as the conditions in which we find ourselves throughout the span of a lifetime, are determined by the kinds of seeds we sow through our thoughts and actions. Just as the seed of one kind of plant produces only that kind of plant, the kinds of actions that we have performed in the past will yield specific results now and later. The law of karma binds us to an ever-repeating cycle of birth, life, death, and rebirth—sowing and reaping, sowing and reaping, sowing and reaping.

2.14 **These [conditions] bring joy or sorrow depending on whether they stem from virtue or vice.**

ते ह्लादपरितापफलाः पुण्यापुण्यहेतुत्वात् ॥

te hlādaparitāpaphalāḥ puṇyāpuṇyahetutvāt

te: these, they
hlāda: delight, pleasure
paritāpa: distress, pain
phala: fruit, result, consequence
puṇya: good, right, meritorious, virtuous
apuṇya: bad, wrong, unmeritorious
hetutva: causality

The intent of any action matters. If we act out of ignorance, can we expect that to lead to wisdom? If we act out of selfishness, can we expect love, harmony, and mutual benefit? If we act out of malice, can we expect anything other than discord and bitterness? But if we act out of goodness, we can expect the benefits of wisdom, love, and tranquility.

What are the hallmarks of virtue and vice? Simply put, virtue takes us toward unity, and vice divides and alienates. Good or virtuous action conducts us toward a well-being and a joy that reflect our own higher nature, while evil behavior leads us into distress.

2.15 **One who is discerning sees all [worldly experience] as suffering, owing to the turmoil of natural forces and to the discomforts of [one's own] lingering impressions, physical and mental pains, and ongoing change.**

परिणामतापसंस्कारदुःखैर्गुणवृत्तिविरोधाच्च दुःखमेव सर्वं विवेकिनः ॥

pariṇāmatāpasaṁskāraduḥkhair guṇavṛttivirodhāc ca duḥkham eva sarvaṁ vivekinaḥ

pariṇāma: transformation, change
tāpa: anguish, anxiety, distress
saṁskāra: impression
duḥkha: existential unease, discomfort, distress, suffering
guṇa: quality, an elemental force of nature
vṛtti: activity, fluctuating state of mind
virodha: opposition, hostility, contradiction, conflict
ca: and
duḥkha: existential unease, discomfort, distress, suffering
eva: indeed, thus
sarva: all
vivekin: one who is discerning or discriminating

This statement is less pessimistic than it first seems. Everything in the outer world and in the inner world of the mind is imperfect. We have to deal with destructive natural forces, human misbehavior, and our own self-made miseries. We carry within ourselves the buried impressions of past joys and sorrows. Sometimes memories of past happiness can trigger painful feelings of present loss. Or the memory of a past trauma can surface to renew the initial horror. The body feels pleasure and pain, and the mind is subject to ever-shifting moods. The happiness of one moment can change in an instant to anger or sadness.

The keyword is *change.* Patañjali has already taught that clinging to what is familiar is one of the five sources of human affliction. We hold on in the face of unstoppable change, and in the end our striving for security proves futile. Over time we progress from youth to old age, we sicken and die. We see those we love and everything we hold dear likewise slip away.

But suffering also has value. It can be an incentive for us to seek something beyond suffering. Who is that "one who is discerning"? One who can distinguish between ordinary experience, with its relative joys and sorrows, and the higher experience of absolute bliss. For such a one, mere human happiness appears scarcely better than misery. Spiritual joy is in a class by itself, and no worldly felicity can ever begin to approach it. When we can discern between what is eternal and unchanging and what is in the constant throes of change, we can rise above the woes of human existence.

2.16 **Future suffering can be prevented.**

हेयं दुःखमनागतम् ॥

heyaṁ duḥkham anāgatam

heya: to be gotten rid of, abandoned, avoided
duḥkha: existential unease, discomfort, distress, suffering
anāgata: yet to come, future

In contrast to the previous *sūtra* this one is clearly optimistic, and to heighten its impact, Patañjali presents it as matter-of-factly as possible. Its simplicity speaks loudly and clearly and opens the door to the deeper insights that follow.

2.17 **The preventable cause [of suffering] is the association of the perceiver with the perceptible.**

द्रष्टृदृश्ययोः संयोगो हेयहेतुः ॥

draṣṭṛdṛśyayoḥ saṁyogo heyahetuḥ

draṣṭṛ: seer, perceiver, the subject who experiences
dṛśya: the seen, the perceptible, the object of experience
saṁyoga: conjunction, connection, contact, association
heya: to be left, quitted, abandoned, relinquished, avoided
hetu: cause

Sūtra 2.6 taught that the sense of an individual, finite self results from mentally identifying with what we perceive. Subjective awareness becomes colored by the perception of what is objective. This association can be prevented through discerning between the supreme witness-Self that we truly are and the ego-self that we merely *think* we are—the one with all the worldly entanglements.

2.18 **Whatever can be known has the qualities of illumination, activity, and inertia and consists of the elements and the senses; its purpose is [to provide both worldly] experience and freedom [from it].**

प्रकाशक्रियास्थितिशीलं भूतेन्द्रियात्मकं भोगापवर्गार्थं दृश्यम् ॥

prakāśakriyāsthitiśīlaṁ bhūtendriyātmakaṁ bhogapavargārthaṁ dṛśyam

prakāśa: radiance, illumination, shining forth
kriyā: action, activity
sthiti: steadiness, inertia
śīla: having the nature (character) of
bhūta: element
indriya: sensory faculty
ātmaka: having the nature of
bhoga: enjoyment, experience
apavarga: emancipation, liberation
artha: purpose, object
dṛśya: that which is seen, the knowable

To break free from the bonds of existence, we first have to understand the nature of existence. "Whatever can be known" is everything that comes before the mind. Every such thing reflects the qualities of the three elemental forces—described here by the words *illumination, activity,* and *inertia.* These account for the existence of every physical object and phenomenon in the universe as well as the mental functions that experience them.

As Patañjali taught in *sūtras* 2.7–9, pleasant experiences lead us to form patterns of thought and behavior based on attraction and the expectation of happiness. Unpleasant or painful experiences create patterns of avoidance or denial. Either way, we fall into patterns of reactive thinking and acting.

So what is the point of this world? As Patañjali sees it, it exists to be experienced, and then for our liberation from that experience. Think about it. The relationship of the knower and the known creates a state of mutual dependence. There is no experience of anything if there is no one to experience it, and there is no one who experiences if there is nothing to experience. That said, experience is bondage. Now think again: without the concept of bondage, how could there be any concept of freedom? Everything that comes before the mind is relative. Even our idea of liberation is an *idea* and not liberation itself.

2.19 **[These] qualities [exist at various] levels: the specific, the general, the abstract, and the potential.**

विशेषाविशेषलिङ्गमात्रालिङ्गानि गुणपर्वाणि ॥

viśeṣāviśeṣaliṅgamātraliṅgāni guṇaparvāṇi

viśeṣa: particularized
aviśeṣa: unparticularized
liṅga: distinctive, characteristic
mātra: only, just
aliṅga: indistinctive, without any distinguishing characteristic
guṇa: quality, an elemental force of nature
parvan: level, stage

Everything from the inert density of a stone to the most rarefied soaring of human intelligence is made of the three universal energies of creation. And these energies, elemental forces, or qualities manifest at four levels.

An apple is not an orange. The two are distinct, and they illustrate what Patañjali means by *specific.* Even so, an apple and an orange are both classified as fruit, and that is a *general* category. You can have a bowl full of apples, pears, oranges, peaches, bananas, pineapples, and so on. Fruit is something material, but it is also something we experience in the *abstract* through a botanical definition—a subtler, conceptual level. You cannot put the concept of fruit in a bowl, but you can hold it in the mind. Finally, the *potential* is that level of existence where the idea is not immediately present to the mind—you are not thinking about fruit in any form, but there is always the possibility that you will. These four terms—*specific, general, abstract, potential*—and the examples that illustrate them should give some idea of the rich complexity of even our most ordinary experience.

It is curious that in *sūtra* 2.18 Patañjali referred to the three elemental forces of creation—a cornerstone of Sāṁkhya philosophy—without using the Sāṁkhya terminology. Instead he used the words *prakāśa* ("illumination"), *kriyā* ("activity"), and *sthiti* ("inertia"). They clearly refer to the three *guṇas,* the "constituent strands" of *prakṛti,* known in Sāṁkhya as *sattva, rajas,* and *tamas.* These terms are untranslatable, and each holds a wealth of meaning. *Sattva* accounts for repose, clarity, wisdom, joy, and serene detachment; *rajas* for motion, restlessness, endeavor, passion, and attachment; *tamas* for inertia, dullness, ignorance, lethargy, and delusion.

2.20 **The perceiver, although pure [consciousness by nature], perceives whatever becomes present to the extent that the power of perception allows.**

द्रष्टा दृशिमात्रः शुद्धोऽपि प्रत्ययानुपश्यः ॥

draṣṭā dṛśimātraḥ śuddho 'pi pratyayānupaśyaḥ

drasṭṛ: seer, perceiver, the subject who experiences
dṛśi: seeing, the power of seeing, perception
mātra: to the extent of, reaching as far as
śuddha: pure
api: although, even though
pratyaya: idea, conception, anything present to awareness
anupaśya: looking upon, perceiving

When Patañjali speaks here of the perceiver, he means the individual subject and not the supreme Self. "Although pure"—although each person is in truth the all-knowing and unlimited being that is the supreme Self—each individual will experience whatever comes before the mind only to the extent that his or her powers of perception and understanding will allow.

2.21 **The perceivable exists only for the sake of the perceiver.**

तदर्थ एव दृश्यस्यात्मा ॥

tadartha eva dṛśyasyātmā

tad: his, of him (the knower)
artha: purpose, sake
eva: indeed, only
dṛśya: the knowable, the object of experience
ātman: essence, nature, character

The value of the world lies in our own experience of it. Apart from the consciousness that perceives it, what other value or meaning could it possibly have?

2.22 **[When] its purpose [is] fulfilled, [the object of experience] vanishes, even though it continues in the shared experience of others.**

कृतार्थं प्रति नष्टमप्यनष्टं तदन्यसाधारणत्वात् ॥

kṛtārthaṁ prati naṣṭam apy anaṣṭaṁ tadanyasādhāraṇa-tvāt

kṛta: accomplished, done, achieved
artha: aim, purpose, motive, reason
prati: toward, with regard to, for
naṣṭa: lost, vanished, destroyed, removed, extinguished
api: also, although, nevertheless
anaṣṭa: not destroyed
tad: that
anya: other
sādhāraṇatva: the state of common (shared) experience

All experience in and of this world is individual. Let us imagine two artists painting in a garden. The minds of both are intent on what they observe as they transfer their impressions to canvas. One artist paints quickly, finishes, and leaves, while the other continues, and two more artists arrive and begin to paint. Thoughts of the flowers no longer occupy the mind of the artist who has accomplished his purpose and left. His mind now becomes occupied with other thoughts, prompted by circumstances outside the garden and new things to do, while the flowers in the garden remain uppermost in the minds of the three artists who are still painting.

On a spiritual level, the consciousness of a person who reaches enlightenment will no longer be concerned with the objects of ordinary experience. Instead, the experience will be one of indescribable Self-awareness, free of all conditioning. Once the activity of the mind has been completely stilled, pure consciousness alone remains, devoid of content. For the enlightened soul, the world as we know it disappears. But for those who are not yet enlightened, the play of the mind's activity goes on unabated, and they will continue to have a shared experience of the manifest world in all its richness and variety.

2.23 **The association of the perceiver and the perceived is the reason for awareness of their distinctive capacities.**

स्वस्वामिशक्त्योः स्वरूपोपलब्धिहेतुः संयोगः ॥

svasvāmiśaktyoḥ svarūpopalabdhihetuḥ saṁyogaḥ

sva: the possessed (the perceived, the known)
svāmi: the possessor, (the perceiver, the knower)
śakti: power, ability, capability, capacity
svarūpa: own-nature, true form, essence
upalabdhi: acquisition, gain, observation, perception, becoming aware
hetu: cause, reason
saṁyoga: conjunction, contact, association, identification

As explained in connection with *sūtra* 2.18, wherever there is a subject (a perceiver), there is also an object (something perceived). The two are relative to each other and in fact help to define each other. Moreover, this association also gives rise in each of us to the sense of a unique individuality, because we are all the creations of our own experience.

2.24 **The cause of this [association] is ignorance.**

तस्य हेतुरविद्या ॥

tasya hetur avidyā

tasya: of it (identification)
hetu: cause
avidyā: ignorance, nescience, unknowing

Ignorance of the primordial unity, which is one's true, original nature, results in the experience of difference in the fractured division of subject and object—of "I and other." Patañjali introduced this fact of ignorance in *sūtra* 2.3 and elaborated on it in the three *sūtras* that followed.

2.25 **With the disappearance of that [ignorance], association no longer exists, and the perceiving [of objects] ceases. Consciousness alone remains.**

तदभावात्संयोगाभावो हानं तद्दृशेः कैवल्यम् ॥

tadabhāvāt saṁyogābhāvo hānaṁ taddṛśeḥ kaivalyam

tad: that, it
abhāva: absence
saṁyoga: conjunction, contact, association, identification
abhāva: absence, non-existence
hāna: the act of abandoning, relinquishing, getting rid of
tad: that
dṛśi: seeing, the power of seeing, consciousness
kaivalya: aloneness, perfect isolation of consciousness from matter (Sāṁkhya definition); absolute unity, singularity (Advaita Vedānta definition)

From what has already been explained, the meaning of this *sūtra* should be self-evident.

2.26 **Undeviating, discerning awareness is the means to bring [ignorance] to an end.**

विवेकख्यातिरविप्लवा हानोपायः ॥

vivekakhyātir aviplavā hānopāyaḥ

viveka: discrimination, discernment
khyāti: knowledge, perception
aviplava: undeviating, undisturbed
hāna: the act of abandoning, relinquishing, getting rid of
upāya: means, method, way

Experience of this world rests on the association or involvement of the perceiver with what is perceived. Once that is in place, we all become the products of our experiences. By discerning awareness, Patañjali means dissociation. At the practical level, if we can gradually overcome our reactivity through the practice of dispassion, we will be less driven—and less shaped—by our experiences. As we proceed to levels of higher insight, the unwavering practice of discernment empowers us ever more to distinguish between appearance and reality.

2.27 **The final goal of that [means, which unfolds] in seven stages, is transcendental knowledge.**

तस्य सप्तधा प्रान्तभूमिः प्रज्ञा ॥

tasya saptadhā prāntabhūmiḥ prajñā

tasya: of that (the means of discerning awareness)
saptadhā: sevenfold, in seven parts
prāntabhūmi: final goal
prajñā: insight, wisdom

Yoga, as we have already learned, is both the means and the goal. Patañjali is about to give us a detailed exposition of the means, the seven levels of practice that lead to the final attainment. Together they make up the eight-limbed yoga.

The pronoun *tasya* means "of that" and refers to the means (*upāya*) just mentioned in the preceding *sūtra. Saptadhā* is an adverb meaning "sevenfold" or "in seven parts." The means unfold in seven stages until the final goal (*prāntabhumi*), the eighth limb of yoga, is reached, culminating in transcendental knowledge (*prajñā*). What could be clearer?

Vyāsa, contrary to Patañjali's systematic presentation, ignores the context and takes *tasya* to mean "his," referring to a previously unmentioned *yogin* (!) and *saptadhā* as an adjective modifying *prajñā*. The result is absurd: "His is a sevenfold transcendental insight." Vyāsa goes on to define this as four stages of conscious discrimination that liberate from external phenomena plus three more that produce freedom from the mind itself. There is no agreement among later commentators over what Vyāsa meant. Georg Feuerstein (page 78) advises caution toward Vyāsa's interpretation, which he concedes may not reflect authentic Yoga tradition.

2.28 **Through practicing the limbs of yoga, as impurities fade away, the light of knowledge [emerges and grows] to discerning awareness.**

योगाङ्गानुष्ठानादशुद्धिक्षये ज्ञानदीप्तिरा विवेकख्यातेः ॥

yogāṅgānuṣṭhānād aśuddhikṣaye jñānadīptir ā vivekakhyāteḥ

yoga: the act of joining, union; means, way, manner, method, application, or concentration of thought
aṅga: limb, member, part
anuṣṭhānā: performance, practice
aśuddhi: impurity
kṣaya: waning, dwindling, diminution, wasting away, destruction
jñāna: knowledge
dīpti: light, lamp
ā: up to, as far as
viveka: discernment, discrimination
khyāti: knowledge, seeing, knowing

Sūtra 2.26 gives discerning awareness as the means to put an end to ignorance. Now we learn how discerning awareness comes about through the structured practice of the stages of yoga. True to form, Patañjali will name those stages in the following *sūtra* and then go on to explain each one.

2.29 **Self-restraint, right observance, posture, regulation of the breath, withdrawal of the senses, concentration, meditation, and meditative union are the eight limbs [of yoga].**

यमनियमासनप्राणायामप्रत्याहारधारणाध्यान-

समाधयोऽष्टावङ्गानि ॥

yamaniyamāsanaprāṇāyāmapratyāhāradhāraṇādhyāna-samādhayo 'ṣṭāv aṅgāni

yama: restraint, abstention
niyama: observance
āsana: posture
prāṇāyāma: breath control, regulation of the breath
pratyāhāra: withdrawal (disengagement) of the senses from external objects
dhāraṇā: concentration (literally, holding, maintaining, keeping)

dhyāna: meditation
samādhi: meditative union, unitary consciousness
aṣṭa: eight
aṅga: limb, member, part

Here they are, simply stated. Discussion of just the first five stages of yoga will take up the rest of this chapter.

A century or two before Patañjali compiled the *Yogasūtra,* a Śaiva author, Lakulīśa (ca. 100–150 CE), detailed his own system of yoga in the *Paśupatasūtra.* He defined yoga as "union with the Lord," attained by the practice of austerities through successive stages. He described this yoga as *aṣṭāṅga,* "eight-limbed" or "having eight parts"—the same term Patañjali was to adopt. The names of the eight stages also are identical, although their order and definition differ somewhat. Here is Lakulīśa's scheme (based on Kanti Chandra Pandey, *An Outline of History of Śaiva Philosophy,* pages 140–141):

1. *niyama:* daily observances
2. *yama:* abstentions
3. *āsana:* posture
4. *prāṇāyāma:* breath-control
5. *pratyāhāra:* withdrawal of the mind from what is external
6. *dhyāna:* concentration with an objective reference
7. *dhāraṇā:* concentration without an objective reference
8. *samādhi:* involuntary concentration

2.30 **Self-restraint [consists of] nonviolence, truthfulness, non-stealing, chastity, and the avoidance of excess.**

अहिंसासत्यास्तेयब्रह्मचर्यापरिग्रहा यमाः ॥

ahiṁsāsatyāsteyabrahmacaryāparigrahā yamāḥ

ahiṁsā: noninjury, nonviolence, doing no harm
satya: truthfulness, veracity
asteya: refraining from stealing, non-stealing
brahmacarya: chastity, continence, celibacy (more broadly, sexual conduct appropriate to one's station in life)
aparigraha: refraining from acquisition or coveting, non-grasping, abstention from greed
yama: restraint, abstention

The first stage of yoga is restraint. Under this heading Patañjali places five disciplines that have to do with our interaction with the surrounding world. These restraints or abstentions are designed to counter the brutish aspects of human nature and to eliminate the negative tendencies and behavior that create disharmony. If we are at odds with the outer world because of other people and circumstances, or if we have qualms about our own conduct or integrity in regard to them, how can we be in a proper frame of mind to cultivate inner stillness?

The practice of nonviolence reins in the tendency toward aggression and leads to benevolence. The practice of truthfulness produces a moral integrity that fosters trust and helps to overcome division. Non-stealing is essential for the same reasons. So is chastity, which here means sexual conduct (or its absence) appropriate to one's circumstances in life; in its highest form it is freedom from the human preoccupation with sex. The fifth restraint, literally "non-grasping," broadly means abstention from greed and the avoidance of excess.

2.31 **These are universal, regardless of birth, place, time, and circumstance; [they constitute] the Great Vow.**

जातिदेशकालसमयानवच्छिन्नाः सार्वभौमा महाव्रतम् ॥

jātideśakālasamayānavacchinnāḥ sārvabhaumā mahāvratam

jāti: birth, life-state, class, caste
deśa: place
kāla: time
samaya: circumstance
anavacchinna: unseparated, not exempted, unconditioned
sārvabhauma: pertaining to all spheres, universal
mahāvrata: great vow

The five restraints appear to be the ethical and moral precepts essential for a healthy society. They are meant to guide all people of every time and place and social standing. Interestingly, they bear a striking resemblance to the latter five of the Judeo-Christian Ten Commandments (Exodus 20:13–17): non-violence corresponds to "Thou shalt not kill"; chastity to "Thou shalt not commit adultery"; non-stealing to "Thou shalt not steal"; truthfulness to "Thou shalt not bear false witness against thy neighbor"; and avoidance of excess to "Thou shalt not covet thy neighbor's house, thou shalt not covet thy neighbor's wife, nor his manservant, nor his maidservant, nor his ox, nor his ass, nor anything that is thy neighbor's."

In the Hindu and Jain traditions these five principles make up what is known as the Great Vow. For the spiritual aspirant they must be observed *consciously* at all times—in action, in speech, and even in thought. Their deeper spiritual import will be disclosed later in *sūtras* 2.35–39.

2.32 **Purity, contentment, ardent discipline, study, and mindfulness of the sacred are the observances.**

शौचसंतोषतपःस्वाध्यायेश्वरप्रणिधानानि नियमाः ॥

śaucasaṁtoṣatapaḥsvādhyāyeśvarapraṇidhānāni niyamāḥ

śauca: cleanliness, purity
saṁtoṣa: contentment
tapas: austerity, self-discipline, ardent cultivation of spiritual discipline
svādhyāya: recitation or study (of sacred texts)
īśvara: lord, ruler, sovereign, master
praṇidhāna: fixing on, respectful attention to, devotion to
niyama: observance

For the spiritual seeker, it is not enough to refrain from harming others, from lying, from stealing, from improper sexual conduct, and from excess, because there is more to spiritual life than good behavior. Besides improving our interactions with the world, we need to look within ourselves.

The second step of yoga is a group of five positive observances, more concerned with the inner rather than with the outer life. These are purity, contentment, ardent disciple, study, and cultivating mindfulness of the sacred. What they entail will become clear in *sūtras* 2.40–45.

In the meantime, before considering the five restraints and the five observances one by one, in the next two *sūtras* Patañjali will instruct us in their general application.

2.33 **When assailed by [negative] thoughts and feelings, one should cultivate their opposites.**

वितर्कबाधने प्रतिपक्षभावनम् ॥

vitarkabādhane pratipakṣabhāvanam

vitarka: cogitation, conjecture, supposition; here, negative thoughts
bādhana: troubling
pratipakṣa: opposite
bhāvana: mental cultivation, creative contemplation

We live in a world marked by pairs of opposites. We experience light and dark, heat and cold, good and evil, calm and agitation, pleasure and misery. How can we turn this play of duality to our advantage?

Whenever a negative thought or feeling takes hold, we should make a conscious effort to think or feel the opposite. If animosity arises, we can counter it with good will. If a desire for something takes hold and causes unrest, we can think of how grateful we are for what we already have. Should feelings of pride arise, we can strive for an attitude of humility.

With sincere and consistent practice unwanted thoughts are gradually displaced, simply crowded out until there is no room left for any of them.

Duality means relativity. The members of any pair of opposites exist only in relation to each other, and they are mutually defining. If there was only light, how could there even be the idea of darkness? If we can succeed in countering every negative thought with a positive one until the positive completely displaces the negative, then what standard of comparison is left even to define what remains as "positive"? Quite simply, we begin by countering the negative with the positive but end by transcending both.

2.34 **Thoughts such as violence and the like—whether they are acted out, instigated, or condoned; whether they arise from greed, anger, or delusion; whether they are mild, moderate, or intense—result in endless ignorance and misery. And so, one should cultivate their opposites.**

वितर्का हिंसादयः कृतकारितानुमोदिता
लोभक्रोधमोहपूर्वका मृदुमध्याधिमात्रा
दुःखाज्ञानानन्तफला इति प्रतिपक्षभावनम् ॥

vitarkā hiṁsādayaḥ kṛtakāritānumoditā lobhakrodha-mohapūrvakā mṛdumadhyādhimātrā duḥkhājñānānanta-phalā iti pratipakṣabhāvanam

vitarka: negative thoughts
hiṁsā: violence, injury
ādi: and so on, and the like, *et cetera*
kṛta: done
kāritā: caused to be done
anumodita: approved, permitted
lobha: greed
krodha: anger
moha: delusion, illusion, confusion, infatuation
pūrvaka: preceded by
mṛdu: mild, slight
madhya: medium
adhimātra: excessive, intense
duḥkha: uneasiness, pain, sorrow, trouble, suffering
ajñāna: ignorance, nescience, unknowing
ananta: unending
phala: fruition, ripening, maturation, end result
iti: thus
pratipakṣa: opposite
bhāvana: mental cultivation, creative contemplation

Any negative thought, feeling, or impulse begins in the mind. If we bear ill will toward another person, maybe we will resort to a mean-spirited remark, a manipulation of events, even physical violence. Maybe we will get someone else to do our dirty work; perhaps we will merely remain passive and allow an injustice to happen and maybe even say it's all right.

Patañjali suggests that our negative feelings may arise out of personal greed, anger, or delusion. Someone possesses something that we want. We resent another's good fortune, thinking it should be ours. Our wishes are thwarted; that makes us angry. We don't fully understand a situation and draw the wrong conclusion. In these ways and in many more, the mind becomes the fertile ground for a toxic harvest.

Negativity can show itself across a broad spectrum from mild annoyance to a simmering anger to a full-blown eruption of rage. We can feel a slight, almost insignificant desire; it can take hold and motivate us to action; it can become intense enough drive us to theft or to corrupt us with an all-consuming greed. Wherever our negative thoughts and actions lie along the spectrum, the end result is disruptive, and we remain subject to misery of one sort or another.

The way out is to be alert for negative impulses, however subtle, and to cultivate their opposites accordingly. The next five *sūtras* will show us what to expect when we succeed.

2.35 **When established in nonviolence, when [fully] present in that, one lets go of [all] hostility.**

अहिंसाप्रतिष्ठायां तत्संनिधौ वैरत्यागः ॥

ahiṁsāpratiṣṭhāyāṁ tatsaṁnidhau vairatyāgaḥ

ahiṁsā: noninjury, nonviolence, doing no harm
pratiṣṭhāya: being established in
tad: that
saṁnidhi: proximity, presence
vaira: enmity, hostility, animosity
tyāga: abandonment, giving up of

When we make the principle of nonviolence a part of our lives, everything changes. We gain a new outlook in which there is no longer any room for animosity or ill will. This new frame of mind affects our behavior at every level—in thought, word, and deed. Gone are resentment, anger, cruelty. Instead we embody kindness, compassion, and benevolence, and those loving attitudes express themselves in everything we think and say and do. Other people notice, and that has a positive effect on them too. Good will is contagious, and the very life of one who is established in nonviolence becomes a blessing to others.

2.36 **When established in truthfulness, [one experiences] a consistency between actions and their results.**

सत्यप्रतिष्ठायां क्रियाफलाश्रयत्वम् ॥

satyapratiṣṭhāyāṁ kriyāphalāśrayatvam

satya: truthfulness, veracity
pratiṣṭhāya: being established in
kriyā: action
phala: fruition, ripening, maturation, end result
āśrayatva: consistency, correspondence

A deceitful person weaves a tangled web and lives with the uncertainty of how things will play out. Events spin out of control when a network of lies comes apart, and carefully plotted deceptions yield unforeseen and unwanted results. Summed up in a couplet: "If one should lie / All goes awry."

The opposite is true for one who is established in truthfulness. Where there is no deception, there is clarity, simplicity, and freedom from complication. There is nothing to spin out of control; rather, actions produce the expected outcome.

The spiritual quest is a quest for truth. It takes us beyond the world of appearances to a greater, abiding reality, which is the truth of our own being. To get there, we must be truthful at every step of the way, because falsity cannot lead to truth.

2.37 **When established in non-stealing, [one finds] all wealth at hand.**

अस्तेयप्रतिष्ठायां सर्वरत्नोपस्थानम् ॥

asteyapratiṣṭhāyāṁ sarvaratnopasthānam

asteya: non-stealing
pratiṣṭhāya: being established in
sarva: all
ratna: jewel, gem; by extension, wealth
upasthāna: approach, a coming into the presence of

Stealing goes contrary to the first two principles of restraint: it causes harm to another and it is dishonest. Any time a craving gets so far out of hand that we would steal, something is very wrong. Stealing is more than an act; it is also the state of mind that drives us to act. And there is more: to crave is to admit that something is lacking, and to admit that something is lacking is to deny our inherent spiritual wholeness. If we allow ourselves to be driven by the wrong idea that owning things can make us happy, we can never know true fulfillment.

By countering such wrong thinking, we can first reach an understanding that we can enjoy things without having to own them. Then we can cultivate gratitude for what we do have and for what we experience. Whatever that may be, it becomes precious. Higher still, when we achieve the freedom from desire, we feel no lack at all and are always satisfied. In that state of mind, we find that "all wealth is at hand."

2.38 **When established in chastity, [one gains] vitality.**

ब्रह्मचर्यप्रतिष्ठायां वीर्यलाभः ॥

brahmacaryapratiṣṭhāyāṁ vīryalābhaḥ

brahmacarya: chastity, continence, celibacy (more broadly, sexual conduct appropriate to one's station in life)
pratiṣṭhāya: being established in
vīrya: vigor, vitality, potency, power
lābha: gain, attainment, acquisition

Sex looms prominent in many, of not most, people's minds and consumes a good deal of energy, whether in thought or deed. In its absence, that energy is available for other, higher pursuits. It's as simple as that.

2.39 **When steadfast in avoiding excess, [one gains] perfect understanding of life's whys and wherefores.**

अपरिग्रहस्थैर्ये जन्मकथंतासंबोधः ॥

aparigrahasthairye janmakathaṁtāsaṁbodhaḥ

aparigraha: refraining from acquisition or coveting, nongrasping, abstention from greed
sthairya: being steady in
janman: birth, existence, life
kathaṁtā: "why-ness," the whys and wherefores
saṁbodha: perfect knowledge or understanding

The word translated here as "avoiding excess" literally means "non-grasping." It can mean taking no more than we need and not depriving others. This meaning illustrates its social value.

Psychologically, non-grasping means not allowing a craving to get out of hand. We all know that one desire leads to another and that to yet another in an endless chain, and all we are left with is restless discontent. Attempts to satisfy greed can lead to all sorts of involvements. That is why non-grasping also means not accepting anything that has strings attached. If we do, we may find ourselves in a state of indebtedness leading to ethical or moral compromise.

The highest value of life is to realize our true being, and that is not possible without "non-grasping." We must be mindful of the endless cravings, excessive consumption, and needless obligations that stand in our way—and let them go. Beyond all the confusion of our ordinary habits lies the clarity of our true being. When right understanding dawns, everything shines in its true perspective, and all those baffling questions about the whys and wherefores of life simply melt away.

2.40 **[Observing] purity [brings] disinclination toward one's own body and the ceasing of contact with [the bodies of] others.**

शौचात्स्वाङ्गजुगुप्सा परैरसंसर्गः ॥

śaucāt svāṅgajugupsā parair asaṁsargaḥ

śauca: cleanliness, purity
sva: own
aṅga: limb, member; here, body
jugupsā: distaste, disgust
para: other
asaṁsarga: nonassociation, cessation of contact

Just as Patañjali cast light on each of the five restraints that make up the first limb of yoga, he will now provide an item-by-item look at the five observances that make up the second limb. In *sūtra* 2.10 he explained that the way to go beyond the disturbances of life is to reverse the flow of consciousness. With the second limb of yoga, our attention begins to turn inward, starting with the cultivation of purity.

Note that Patañjali's first thoughts on purity relate to our attitude toward the physical body. The body exists in the outer world. It is made of the same material elements as other physical objects, and when we identify with it, we identify not with consciousness but with matter. This runs contrary to the whole point of yoga, which teaches that our true being is consciousness, or spirit.

Where does purity fit in? According to the Indian views of evolution, the whole of nature evolves from the subtle to the gross through a series of cosmic principles. The subtlest of all created things is the light of human intelligence; the grossest is dense physical matter. In evolutionary terms, matter is the end of the line. When we identify with the physical body and think this is who we are, we place ourselves in a condition of the greatest limitation. The body has a defined volume that occupies a certain small amount of space, it can be present in only one place at any time, and its properties and actions are strictly determined by the laws of nature. The Śaiva tradition, which formulated the idea of the eight limbs of yoga, looks on this limitation as impurity.

This understanding is not puritanical. Patañjali is not a prude; he does not say that to identify with the body is immoral. He does not call for the unhealthy repression of natural impulses but only for a simple change of attitude: it is better not to identify with the most limited and limiting part of who we think we are. It is better to stop thinking of ourselves as physical beings and to identify instead with the highest expression of human awareness, which is the pure power of right understanding. Only then can we make the final leap into the fullness of Self-knowledge, which is beyond matter and even beyond thought.

2.41 **Moreover, the purification of the mind [brings about] cheerfulness, focused concentration, mastery of the senses, and the fitness for Self-knowledge.**

सत्त्वशुद्धिसौमनस्यैकाग्र्येन्द्रियजयात्मदर्शनयोग्य-
त्वानि च ॥

sattvaśuddhisaumanasyaikāgryendriyajayātmadarśana-
yogyatvāni ca

sattva: the highest aspect of human intelligence, buddhi
śuddhi: purity, purification
saumanasya: cheerfulness
ekāgrya: one-pointedness
indriya: sensory faculty
jaya: mastery, control
ātman: Self
darśana: (direct) seeing
yogyatva: fitness, qualification
ca: and

Once we turn our interest away from the body, we can begin the inner purification of the mind. No longer identified so strongly with our physical limitations, we feel a natural cheerfulness that is, as yet, only a hint of the infinite joy that awaits us. With fewer external distractions, our attention becomes more easily focused, and all the sensations of sound, touch, sight, taste, and smell lessen their hold. A dawning sense of empowerment tells is that, yes, we *can* attain enlightenment.

2.42 **From contentment [comes] unsurpassed happiness.**

संतोषादनुत्तमः सुखलाभः ॥

saṁtoṣād anuttamaḥ sukhalābhaḥ

saṁtoṣa: contentment
anuttama: unexcelled, highest
sukha: happiness, well-being, joy
lābha: gain, attainment, acquisition

Letting go of cravings, we want for nothing. As *sūtra* 2.37 put it, "all wealth is at hand." Now Patañjali tells of an even deeper experience. The contentment of which he speaks here is not achieved by the act of letting go—that was only the first step. Real contentment is the knowledge of our innate wholeness, already present. It has merely been covered over by the many desires arising out of our interactions with the world—of wanting to make "ours" what is "out there." Contentment is, therefore, not about letting go of desires but about maintaining a frame of mind in which they do not even arise.

2.43 **Because impurities fade away through ardent discipline, [one gains] refinement of the body and the senses.**

कायेन्द्रियसिद्धिरशुद्धिक्षयात्तपसः ॥

kāyendriyasiddhir aśuddhikṣayāt tapasaḥ

kāya: body
indriya: sensory faculty
siddhi: refinement, perfection

aśuddhi: impurity
kṣaya: waning, dwindling, diminution, wasting away, destruction
tapas: ardent spiritual discipline

This *sūtra* can be taken in two simple ways. The first is that through sincere, enthusiastic self-discipline, the limitations of body and mind—the so-called impurities—fade away. As they cease to occupy our awareness, they become less able to make an effect. In their absence, the body and senses become fit instruments for the practice of yoga.

The second interpretation goes further. Again, through sincere, enthusiastic self-discipline, the limitations of body and mind—the so-called impurities—fade away. In their absence, the body and senses have served their purpose. They have allowed us to experience our human existence, but now it is time to move on toward the higher experience of the Self.

Both interpretations are based on straightforward readings of the word *siddhi.* In the first, *siddhi* means "efficacy." In the second it means "fulfillment" or "accomplishment." Neither reading is to be found among the classical commentators. They all follow Vyāsa, who took *siddhi* in the highly specialized sense of paranormal or occult powers.

The word *tapas,* rendered here as "ardent discipline," is usually translated as "austerity," "penance," or "mortification." But should yogic practice be a grim affair? Can self-imposed discomfort be the path to lasting peace and blessedness? The basic meaning of *tapas* is "warmth," "heat," or "burning." In the traditional view, fire burns away impurities, and *tapas* is therefore a purifying discipline. This same idea of heat and burning is conveyed by the word *ardor,* from the Latin word for flame. Discipline may be understood initially in the sense of austerity—of controlling one's impulses—but *ardor* means that we should bring passion, eagerness, and enthusiasm to our practice. With a positive and joyful attitude our "discipline" is more likely to yield positive results. The Mahābhārata (12.250.4) defines the highest *tapas* as "one-pointedness of the mind and senses on a single object." So we see that *tapas* stretches all the way from initial self-restraint to profound contemplation.

2.44 **From the study [of sacred teaching, one reaches] communion with the chosen aspect of the Divine.**

स्वाध्यायादिष्टदेवतासंप्रयोगः ॥

svādhyāyād iṣṭadevatāsaṁprayogaḥ

svādhyāya: recitation or study (of sacred texts)
iṣṭadevatā: chosen deity
saṁprayoga: connection, contact, communion

The word for *study* traditionally means the recitation of sacred texts. Here it means a personal study that takes us beyond conventional religion—a private, solitary contemplation of the sacred texts, free of surrounding distractions and open to ever deepening insight. But remember, at this stage we are only communing mentally with our *ideas* of the Divine.

2.45 **Through [constant] mindfulness of the sacred, [one reaches] the beatitude of meditative union.**

समाधिसिद्धिरीश्वरप्रणिधानात् ॥

samādhisiddhir īśvarapraṇidhānāt

samādhi: meditative union, unitary consciousness
siddhi: perfection
īśvarapraṇidhāna: directing the mind Godward, fixing the mind on the Supreme Being, profound contemplation of the Divine

Through study we learn about the experiences of others who attained direct knowledge of the highest truth, but we have to know that truth for ourselves. With the fifth observance we carry on a profound interaction with that higher aspect of consciousness that Patañjali first introduced in *sūtra* 1.23—the one we may choose to call God, the Supreme Being, or the Divine. By directing the mind continually Godward, by fixing it there, by becoming fully established in the divine presence, we ultimately become absorbed in it. Long before Patañjali, in the Muṇḍakopaniṣad (3.2.8–9), an earlier seer proclaimed:

> Just as the flowing rivers, leaving behind their names and forms, merge into the ocean, so does the knowing one, freed from name and form, attain the all-transcending reality. Whoever knows the supreme Brahman becomes Brahman.

That goal still lies ahead. So far Patañjali has only explained the first two stages of yoga. It is time to move on to the third.

2.46 **Posture [should be] steady and comfortable.**

स्थिरसुखमासनम् ॥

sthirasukham āsanam

sthira: steady
sukha: at ease, comfortable
āsana: posture

Most people who think of yoga immediately think of posture. Unlike the yogic postures and exercises so popular today, which many engage in for physical and mental well-being, the posture that Patañjali speaks of has one purpose: to aid us in meditation.

The first limb of yoga, with its five practices, addressed our relationship to the outer world. The second limb indicated five ways to an inner change of attitude. Now that we are ready to sit for meditation, we must consider the proper conditions. Patañjali names only two—steadiness and comfort. The point is to forget our identification with the body, and the best way to do that is not to have the body call attention to itself.

Vyāsa, naming thirteen specific postures, goes far beyond this *sūtra's* simple requirements. An earlier text that would have been known to Patañjali, the Śvetāśvataropaniṣad (2.8, 10), has this to say:

> Holding the body steady with chest, neck, and head aligned, then mentally directing the senses into the heart, one who is

wise may cross over every fear-laden current on the raft of Brahman. … In a clean and level place, free of pebbles, fire, and dust, free of noise and dampness, calming to the mind, and not displeasing to the eye—here, sheltered from the wind and retiring into solitude, one should concentrate the mind.

2.47 **Relaxing of effort [should be accompanied by a feeling of] convergence with the Infinite.**

प्रयत्नशैथिल्यानन्तसमापत्तिभ्याम् ॥

prayatnaśaithilyānantasamāpattibhyām

prayatna: effort, endeavor, exertion
śaithilya: relaxation, decrease
ananta: endless, infinite
samāpatti: "falling together," convergence; in Yoga philosophy, assuming a particular state or condition, thought transformation, engrossment, mental absorption

When we first sit to meditate, we may be very aware of our physical form, of the amount of space it occupies, of its boundaries, and of being confined by it to a specific place at a specific time. The way to overcome this is to forget the body.

Besides sitting still in a comfortable position, we need to *relax*. Think about it: making an effort not to do anything is a contradiction in terms! With effortless relaxation, the sense of physical limitation falls away, and our awareness is free to connect with something else—something that was there all along, only hidden. We may get an inkling that our awareness can expand to infinity.

2.48 **Then one is no longer assailed by [the play of] opposites.**

ततो द्वंद्वानभिघातः ॥

tato dvaṁdvānabhighātaḥ

tatas: then, consequently
dvaṁdva: pair (of opposites)
anabhighāta: unassailability, nonaffliction

The pairs of opposites that we experience through the senses include all the physical sensations that the eyes, ears, nose, tongue, and skin transmit to the mind. Ordinarily we react to heat and cold, to light and dark, to sound and silence, and they cause comfort or discomfort. Once we manage to suspend the mind's association with the body, those sensations vanish and leave us open to higher experiences.

2.49 **Once this is achieved, [there follows] breath control, [attention to] the division of the inward and outward flow.**

तस्मिन्सति श्वासप्रश्वासयोर्गतिविच्छेदः प्राणायामः ॥

tasmin sati śvāsapraśvāsayor gativicchedaḥ prāṇāyāmaḥ

tasmin: in this
sati: being
śvāsa: inhalation, in-breath
praśvāsa: exhalation, out-breath
gati: movement, motion, manner of going, flow
viccheda: division, separation, interruption, discontinuance
prāṇāyāma: breath-control, regulation of the breath

Once we have stilled the outer movements of the body and are settling into a comfortable, relaxed position, it is time to turn our attention to the breath that animates the body. The fourth limb of yoga focuses on this outward sign of life. We are to make that the focus of attention, observing its flow in and out.

Have you ever noticed that if you are physically active—running or exercising, for example—or stressed, your breathing becomes heavy and irregular? It is equally true that if you are relaxed, not just physically but also mentally, the flow of the breath becomes gentle, even, and shallow. Later on, in states of deep concentration, you may find that you are hardly breathing at all, and that this has occurred naturally without your giving it a thought.

2.50 **The movement [of breath] is outward, inward, and suspended. [Its division], beheld in terms of place, time, and number, is subtle and far-reaching.**

बाह्याभ्यन्तरस्तम्भवृत्तिर्देशकालसंख्याभिः परिदृष्टो दीर्घसूक्ष्मः ॥

bāhyābhyantarastambhavṛttir deśakālasaṁkhyābhiḥ paridṛṣṭo dīrghasūkṣmaḥ

bāhya: external
abhyantara: internal
stambha: stopped
vṛtti: activity, function, mode of conduct, state, condition
deśa: point, spot, place, location
kāla: time, a space of time, duration
saṁkhya: number, calculation, deliberation, reasoning
paridṛṣṭa: observed, beheld, looked at
dīrgha: long; here, far-reaching
sūkṣma: subtle

Watching the flow of breath in and out is only the first step. The fuller meaning of breath control and its benefits will become clear in this and the three *sūtras* that follow.

As we watch the flow of breath, Patañjali wants us to notice that it has not two but three phases. The inflow and the outflow are obvious enough, but have you ever stopped to think about that still point where the direction reverses? Indeed, the breath naturally has three phases. The previous *sūtra* defined breath control as a mental division of the flow, and this observation of its three phases is division by number.

Division should also be by time. An in-breath takes a certain amount of time; so does an out-breath. But the turning-point is timeless.

The third division refers to place. We have calmed the mind

by watching the breath flow steadily in and out. We have focused attention on the timeless point. Now, the physical places of reference lie twelve fingers' breadth below the tip of the nose, where the out-breath ends, and within the heart, where the in-breath ends. At either terminus of this arc there is no activity, only stillness.

Vyāsa understands *prāṇāyāma* merely as the natural suspension of breath that occurs in the absence of inhalation and exhalation. He writes nothing more than that. Vācaspati Miśra and later commentators suggest an elaborate system of exercises—breathing in, breathing out, and holding the breath for so many counts in certain mathematical proportions.

The broader definition of the word *prāṇa* is "vital force," a principle with five aspects. These are: *prāṇa,* the outgoing breath; *apāna,* the incoming breath, responsible also for elimination; *samāna,* the internal energy that governs digestion, assimilation, and circulation; *vyāna,* which presides over the nervous system, speech, and conscious action; and *udāna,* which promotes growth, maintains bodily heat, and aids in the soul's departure from the body at death. The five are all interconnected and finely balanced aspects of metabolism. It must be emphasized that forced and artificial manipulation of the breath can cause irreversible damage to the nervous system.

Just as Patañjali did not recommend any particular yogic postures, he does not suggest any particular breathing exercises. His *prāṇāyāma* is purely mental and aimed at directing us to a higher spiritual insight. That will become abundantly clear in the next three *sūtras.*

2.51 **Surpassing the scope of the outward and inward [breaths is] the fourth [state of consciousness].**

बाह्याभ्यन्तरविषयाक्षेपी चतुर्थः ॥

bāhyābhyantaraviṣayākṣepī caturthaḥ

bāhya: external
abhyantara: internal
viṣaya: sphere, range, region, domain

ākṣepin: going beyond, surpassing, transcending
caturtha: fourth

The out-breath and the in-breath become symbols of human existence in time. Focusing away from time and toward timelessness gives a hint of something higher. Hindu tradition calls this "the fourth," because it lies beyond our normal awareness in the states of waking, dreaming, and deep sleep.

2.52 **In consequence [of recognizing this], the veiling of the light [of consciousness] diminishes.**

ततः क्षीयते प्रकाशावरणम् ॥

tataḥ kṣīyate prakāśāvaraṇam

tatas: from that, in consequence of that
kṣīyate: decreases, diminishes, weakens, wastes away
prakāśa: a shining forth, radiance, illumination; self-luminous consciousness
āvaraṇa: the act of covering, concealing, hiding

When we feel an intimation of a consciousness superior to any awareness we normally have while awake, dreaming, or sleeping, what is happening? The ignorance that normally veils our own higher awareness begins to weaken.

The Self is self-luminous; it shines constantly in full glory, only we have failed to notice because our minds are occupied with other things. Just as the sun shines brightly above a dense layer of clouds but we receive only a fraction of its light, the light of the Self shines from within, ever untouched by the veils of unknowing that dim our awareness.

2.53 **And the cognitive mind becomes fit for the stages of concentration [that follow].**

धारणासु च योग्यता मनसः ॥

dhāraṇāsu ca yogyatā manasaḥ

dhāraṇā: an act of holding the mind; concentration
ca: and
yogyatā: fitness, qualification
manas: cognitive mind, receptor of sensory stimuli

The light, shining brightly, illuminates every corner, if even for only an instant. Here Patañjali is referring to a particular "corner" or part of the mind, specifically to that part of our field of awareness that receives and processes the information coming in through the senses. We are ready to move on in search of a better understanding of how we perceive the outer world so that our perception will cease to be an obstacle.

2.54 **When the sensory faculties disengage from their [external] objects and assimilate to the nature of the mind, [this is called] withdrawal of the senses.**

स्वविषयासंप्रयोगे चित्तस्वरूपानुकार इवेन्द्रियाणां प्रत्याहारः ॥

svaviṣayāsaṁprayoge cittasvarūpānukāra ivendriyāṇāṁ pratyāhāraḥ

sva: own
viṣaya: object, subject matter, content, domain
asaṁprayoga: not coming into contact with, disconnection, disjunction, dissociation, detachment
citta: mind
svarūpa: own-form, essence, true nature
anukāra: imitation, resemblance
iva: in the same manner, just so, indeed
indriya: sensory faculty (the five capacities of hearing, feeling, seeing, tasting, and smelling)
pratyāhāra: withdrawal

The withdrawal of the senses goes deeper than you might think. I see an apple; I close my eyes and do not see it. That's not what the fifth limb of yoga is about. The disconnection takes place deeper inside, where the faculties of perception come into contact not with their objects but with the mind. We need to know more about how the process of knowing works.

I see an apple, but do I really? The physical apple does not come into direct contact with my mind. It is the perception of the apple, not the apple itself, that I experience. I see the apple because information about its form and color flow in through the sense of sight. I touch the apple and know that it is smooth and firm because of the information transmitted by my ability to feel. I enjoy the fragrance of the apple because of my ability to smell, and so on. But my multidimensional experience of the apple consists entirely of sensations, and those are modifications that become present to the mind. In brief, for each of us the world exists only in our experience of it, and that experience takes place in the mind.

Therefore, if we wish to withdraw awareness from the outer world, we must disengage internally, where the connection of the senses to the mind takes place.

2.55 **From this arises complete mastery over the senses.**

ततः परमा वश्यतेन्द्रियाणाम् ॥

tataḥ paramā vaśyatendriyāṇām

tatas: then, from this, consequently
parama: supreme
vaśyatā: control, mastery
indriya: sensory faculty

This means that any sense perception, which is by nature a form of mental activity, can be stopped at will. By mastering the fifth limb of yoga, we master the level of perceptual knowledge, which is experience of the external world. The higher, internal levels of knowledge will be the focus of the remaining limbs of yoga, following immediately in the next chapter.

CHAPTER 3

3.1 **Concentration is holding the mind in [one] place.**

देशबन्धश्चित्तस्य धारणा ॥

deśabandhaś cittasya dhāraṇā

> deśa: point, place
> bandha: binding
> citta: mind (with its functions of perceiving, thinking, imagining, intending, deciding, memory, and self-definition)
> dhāraṇā: concentration, holding, maintaining

The first limb of yoga was about having a correct relationship with the outer world. The next four limbs took us gradually inward, but even the fifth limb, which is about turning attention away from sensory experiences, still involves the idea that an outer world exists. We are just trying not to perceive it. The sixth limb marks the turning point, because now we are asked to redirect our attention, not *away from* the outer, but *toward* the inner. There is a subtle difference, because now the effects of the outer—of anything related to the senses of hearing, touching, seeing, smelling, or tasting—should be absent from the mind.

The Sanskrit name for the sixth limb of yoga, translated here as "concentration," literally means "holding." The *sūtra* tells us first to redirect our attention to a single inner point and then to hold it there. It is worth noting that the English word *attention* comes from the Latin *attinere,* which also means "to hold to."

The chapter break that occurs between the fifth and sixth limbs of yoga seems somewhat peculiar, given that all eight form a unit. However, this break marks the turning point in the flow of consciousness, away from the outer world of objects and toward the inner realm of pure subjective awareness. It is that inner realm that the third chapter explores.

The *Yogasūtra*'s four chapters bear titles that are not Patañjali's own. The designations *Samādhipāda, Sādhanapāda, Vibhūtipāda,* and *Kaivalyapāda* were added by a later hand. For that reason they are not employed in this book. It should be noted also that the word *vibhūti,* meaning "expansion" but usually taken to mean occult powers, occurs nowhere in Patañjali's text.

3.2 **There that state of singular focus [becomes] meditation.**

तत्र प्रत्ययैकतानता ध्यानम् ॥

tatra pratyayaikatānatā dhyānam

tatra: there, therein
pratyaya: idea, conception, anything present to awareness
ekatānatā: the state of singular focus
dhyāna: meditation

After attaining concentration, the next step is to allow no other thought to arise. Meditation is defined as the uninterrupted flow of thought to the object of attention, traditionally likened to an unbroken flow of oil or honey poured from one vessel to another.

The wording of this *sūtra* links concentration to meditation. At first our attempts to concentrate are intermittent. We usually find our thoughts wandering after only a short while. But once we succeed in holding the mind to a single point, *there*—in that state—concentration becomes meditation. The difference between the two lies only in duration and intensity.

3.3 **When that [meditation] itself shines forth as the sole object [present to the mind], as if devoid [even] of the mind's own nature, [that is] meditative union.**

तदेवार्थमात्रनिर्भासं स्वरूपशून्यमिव समाधिः ॥

tad evārthamātranirbhāsaṁ svarūpaśūnyam iva samādhiḥ

tad: that (meditation)
eva: indeed
artha: object
mātra: alone
nirbhāṣa: shining forth
svarūpa: own-form, essence
śunya: empty, devoid of
iva: as if
samādhi: meditative union, unitary consciousness

The experience continues to deepen until the meditative state itself becomes the sole "object" present to the mind. The experience crowds out any sense of even the mind's presence. The mind as we know it is pushed aside, and the state that results is one of meditative union. As we learned in the first chapter, this eighth limb of yoga is of two degrees, described as "with seed" and "without seed," indicating whether the experience is one of partial identification or complete identity.

You may have observed that the initial stage of holding the mind involves will and requires a degree of effort. When concentration becomes prolonged and deepened, it shades into meditation, and as the flow of consciousness becomes less effortful and more spontaneous, it leads to meditative union.

Translating the technical terms of yoga is difficult, because there are no English equivalents. Since this book is meant to be a simple and practical guide, the Sanskrit terms do not appear in the primary level of commentary. However, it is arguable whether the word *concentration* is any better than the word *dhāraṇā* or that *meditation* adequately conveys the idea of *dhyāna* or that *absorption* or *union* come anywhere near to the full meaning of *samādhi.* The same can be said of the next term we will encounter, *saṁyama.*

3.4 **[Practicing] the three as one [is called] total engagement.**

त्रयमेकत्र संयमः ॥

trayam ekatra saṁyamaḥ

traya: triad, group of three
ekatra: as one
saṁyama: total mental engagement, full comprehension

"Total engagement" consists of practicing the final three limbs of yoga together in reference to a single object of thought. This means 1) directing attention to a specific point and holding it there, 2) contemplating in uninterrupted stillness until 3) reaching a penetration whereby the object of contemplation becomes fully experienced—known, we might say, "from the inside out." Note, however, that such full comprehension of any object is not the final goal of yoga, because it is not the experience of the self-aware Self.

The term *saṁyama* has no English counterpart, and all translations, including "total engagement" and "full comprehension," fall short. The root *yam* has a range of meaning that includes to "sustain, hold, support; extend, expand; hold back, restrain, check, control; offer, confer, bestow." The prefix *sam-*, like the Latin *con-* and the Greek *syn-*, means "with" or "together with" and can denote union, thoroughness, intensity, or completeness. "Total engagement" is a workable rendering of *saṁyama,* provided that we remember that the Sanskrit term also implies a degree of understanding well beyond the range of ordinary knowledge.

3.5 **Through its mastery [comes] insightful vision.**

तज्जयात्प्रज्ञालोकः ॥

tajjayāt prajñālokaḥ

tad: it, that
jaya: mastery, victory over
prajñā: wisdom, intelligence, knowledge
āloka: seeing, beholding, vision, light, splendor

By mastering the practice of total engagement, we gain power over whatever is our focus. That is the meaning behind the maxim that "knowledge is power." The word *mastery* further suggests that our practice cannot be a casual affair. To be totally engaged depends on being fully dedicated.

3.6 **Its application [proceeds] in stages.**

तस्य भूमिषु विनियोगः ॥

tasya bhūmiṣu viniyogaḥ

tasya: its
bhūmi: stage
viniyoga: application, employment

We can't just turn our attention to something and expect instantaneous results. Total engagement doesn't happen all at once but is reached step by step. You wouldn't study the first and last parts of a textbook, skip the middle, and expect to have mastered the subject. Likewise total engagement requires bringing the sixth, seventh, and eighth limbs of yoga together in a single process. It allows for no shortcuts.

3.7 **[These] three are internal [in relation] to the previous [limbs of yoga].**

त्रयमन्तरङ्गं पूर्वेभ्यः ॥

trayam antaraṅgaṁ pūrvebhyaḥ

traya: triad, group of three
antar: internal
aṅga: limb, part, stage
pūrva: previous

Patañjali affirms that the limbs of yoga represent a progressive journey inward. With the sixth limb, concentrating on a purely internal focal point, we take leave of the outer world.

3.8 **Yet even these limbs are outside the seedless [state of consciousness].**

तदपि बहिरङ्गं निर्बीजस्य ॥

tad api bahiraṅgaṁ nirbījasya

tad: that (triad)
api: even
bahis: external
aṅga: limb, part, stage
nirbīja: seedless

Even the higher levels of human consciousness are still just that—human consciousness. Only by going beyond the highest reach of human intelligence do we reach the ultimate, or seedless absorption, which is realization of the true Self, distinct from anything in our human experience.

3.9 **When the mind conforms to outgoing activity, there is manifestation; [when it conforms to inner] stillness, [there is the] absence [of manifestation]. The mind's association with [even] an instant of stillness [marks] progress toward stillness.**

व्युत्थाननिरोधसंस्कारयोरभिभवप्रादुर्भावौ
निरोधक्षणचित्तान्वयो निरोधपरिणामः ॥

vyutthānanirodhasaṁskārayor abhibhavaprādurbhāvau
nirodhakṣaṇacittānvayo nirodhapariṇāmaḥ

vyutthāna: rising, the experience of the phenomenal world
nirodha: restraint, check, control, stilling
saṁskāra: mental impression; (in Buddhist usage) a conforming of the mind (such as to the external world)
abhibhava: non-manifestation
prādurbhāva: external manifestation
nirodha: restraint, check, control, stilling
kṣaṇa: instant of time, moment
citta: mind (with its functions of perceiving, thinking, imagining, intending, deciding, memory, and self-definition)

anvaya: association, connection
nirodha: restraint, check, control, stilling
pariṇāma: transformation, change, development, evolution

The key to this *sūtra* is found at the beginning of the first chapter, where Patañjali said that yoga is the stilling of the mind's activity (1.2), that to achieve it is to abide in our true nature (1.3), and that otherwise we identify with the objects and events of the surrounding world (1.4).

How does this work? As we think, so we become—that's the essential message, and it is a truth expressed in many religious traditions. If we can focus sufficiently on stillness, we will become still. It's all a matter of where the mind is in the moment and of extending the moment.

3.10 **The [mind's] calm flow [comes] out of the latent impression [of stillness].**

तस्य प्रशान्तवाहिता संस्कारात् ॥

tasya praśāntavāhitā saṁskārāt

tasya: its (the mind's)
praśānta: calm, quiet, tranquil, composed
vāhitā: flow
saṁskāra: latent impression

Repeated effort at contemplative stillness, like every other experience, leaves its mark on the mind. It is the sum total of these mental impressions that forms our character and heightens our abilities. It is only natural that when the mind grows accustomed to an inner quietude, those impressions will prevail and aid us in our further endeavor.

3.11 **With the [linked] fading of distraction and the rise of a singular focus, the mind evolves toward meditative union.**

सर्वार्थतैकाग्रतयोः क्षयोदयौ चित्तस्य
समाधिपरिणामः ॥

sarvārthataikāgratayoḥ kṣayodayau cittasya
samādhipariṇāmaḥ

sarva: all
arthatā: objectivity
ekāgratā: one-pointedness
kṣaya: waning, dwindling, diminution, wasting away, destruction
udaya: rising up, manifestation
citta: mind, the individual's field of awareness
samādhi: meditative union, unitary consciousness
pariṇāma: transformation, change, development, evolution

As we manage to turn the mind away from all the sights and sounds and other matters of everyday living, we notice that their influence weakens and gives way to engagement with a single point. When one state arises, the other falls. We might call this the "seesaw effect." Recognizing that, we can choose either to identify with the objects and events around us or to aspire to the experience of our true nature.

3.12 **Again, when sameness is present in [both] the rising and falling [thoughts], the mind moves toward one-pointedness.**

ततः पुनः शान्तोदितौ तुल्यप्रत्ययौ
चित्तस्यैकाग्रतापरिणामः ॥

tataḥ punaḥ śāntoditau tulyapratyayau
cittasyaikāgratāpariṇāmaḥ

tatas: then
punar: again
śānta: peaceful, subdued
udita: rsing up, manifest
tulya: equal

pratyaya: idea, conception, anything present to awareness
citta: mind, the individual's field of awareness
ekāgratā: one-pointedness
pariṇāma: transformation, change, development, evolution

Here Patañjali defines one-pointedness. Thinking that is focused exclusively on a single object is not thinking that has stopped. Rather, thinking of any kind is a process made of separate, succeeding instants. Only when every succeeding instant is identical to the one before does our attention seem unchanging or one-pointed.

3.13 **This [same principle conversely] explains changes of form, characteristic, and condition in the perception of objects.**

एतेन भूतेन्द्रियेषु धर्मलक्षणावस्थापरिणामा
व्याख्याताः ॥

etena bhūtendriyeṣu dharmalakṣaṇāvasthāpariṇāmā vyākhyātāḥ

etena: by this
bhūta: that which exists, element, object
indriya: sensory capacity (seeing, hearing, feeling, tasting, smelling; the plural denotes all five)
dharma: form (that which is established or firm)
lakṣaṇa: characteristic, attribute, quality
avasthā: state, condition
pariṇāma: transformation, change, development, evolution
vyākhyāta: explained

When the mind is held in one-pointed attention, it is unaware of any difference or change, because nothing else is present for comparison. Conversely, when the mind is not singly focused but engages with one thing after another, it becomes aware of change.

Patañjali mentions changes of form, characteristic, and condition. An apple begins life as an apple blossom. When pollinated by a bee, the flower begins to change into a fruit. That is a change of form. The unripe apple is sour; the ripe apple will be sweet. That is a change of characteristic. After the apple has ripened, if we fail to eat it, it will eventually rot away. That is a change of condition, from existing to not existing. Everything in the material world is subject to these kinds of change. At every moment, whatever comes to our attention is in some stage of transformation.

Besides the changes in objects, there are changes in how we perceive them. Why? Because our perceptions also are objects—mental objects. So are the thoughts that grow out of our perceptions and are held momentarily in the mind. Like the apple—but more quickly—a thought arises, becomes present, and is gone, transforming all the while.

3.14 **Whatever has qualities is subject to the laws that govern them, in the past, present, and future.**

शान्तोदिताव्यपदेश्यधर्मानुपाती धर्मी ॥

śāntoditāvyapadeśyadharmānupātī dharmī

śānta: abated, ceased, the past
udita: arisen, the present
avyapadeśya: unnamed, the future
dharma: manner, prescribed course, conduct, law
anupātin: following as a consequence or result
dharmin: the bearer of any characteristic or attribute

Everything in the creation is subject to a universal law of cause and effect and operates accordingly. This was as true yesterday as it is today and will be tomorrow. It applies equally to the realm of physical matter and to the inner domain of the mind.

3.15 **A difference in the sequence [of properties] accounts for the changing nature [of objects].**

क्रमान्यत्वं परिणामान्यत्वे हेतुः ॥

kramānyatvaṁ pariṇāmānyatve hetuḥ

krama: going, proceeding, course, sequence
anyatva: otherness, differentiation
pariṇāma: transformation, change, development, evolution
anyatva: otherness, difference
hetu: cause, reason

That single principle of cause and effect gives rise to any number of individual manifestations, all creating the world we know and the many ways in which we know it. How a thing appears depends on the momentary patterning of the elemental properties from which it is made. Because those are in constant motion, our perceptions are in fact dynamic successions of change, each sequence of elements giving rise to a particular manifestation that becomes present to the mind.

3.16 **Through total engagement with the three changes [of form, characteristic, and condition comes] knowledge of the past and future.**

परिणामत्रयसंयमादतीतानागतज्ञानम् ॥

pariṇāmatrayasaṁyamād atītānāgatajñānam

pariṇāma: transformation, change, development, evolution
traya: triad, group of three
saṁyama: total mental engagement, full comprehension
atīta: past, bygone
anāgata: future, not yet come
jñāna: knowledge

Knowing the principles of change allows us to look at something in the present and to make inferences about its past and predictions about its future. This *sūtra* is not about visiting a psychic to learn what we were doing in a previous lifetime or to find out what the future holds in store. It is a statement of fact concerning our powers of observation and reason.

Time belongs to the natural realm, to the world of relativity, where past, present, and future all exist only in relation to one another. The present is, well, present—here and now. But the present we know is both the effect of the past and the cause of the future. With penetrating awareness of all the distinctions in the present, we gain a broader knowledge of their connection to what was and is yet be.

Spiritual truth is eternal and unchanging, but the conditions of the natural world are changing all the time. To be liberated from worldly existence, we must first understand what we wish to be liberated from. There is great truth to the adage that "knowledge is power." When we understand something fully—be it a physical phenomenon or the working of the mind—we can use it to our advantage.

The purpose of *sūtras* 3.16–48 is to make us aware of the powers of the mind so that we can use them optimally. It is noteworthy that *sūtra* 3.37 cautions that the outward engagement of the mind does not lead to liberation but to its opposite. As the Sāṁkhya philosophy defines it, liberation is the total *disengagement* of consciousness from matter, not its involvement.

Here we come to the delicate matter of interpreting these *sūtras* rationally. In the very next *sūtra* Patañjali will speak of the confusion of word, object, and concept. Words can be taken in more than one sense and at more than one level of meaning. The classical commentators often go for readings that make fantastic claims of occult or paranormal powers. These same *sūtras* can be read as metaphorical statements that dispel any suggestion of the supernatural and speak instead of genuine mystical experience.

As we approach the *sūtras* ahead, let's keep in mind the premise that there is no supernatural—only parts of the natural that we do not yet fully understand. Although some of what Patañjali is about to present is mistaken as occult or paranormal, the experiences he describes arise not from overriding the laws of nature but from intensive engagement with them. Moreover, everything Patañjali has presented thus far is firmly grounded in rationality; why should these *sūtras* be any different?

Many of the powers that Patañjali describes as extraordinary are powers that we take for granted today, not because of yogic discipline but because of technology. In a sense Patañjali was prophetic, although that was not his aim. Because brilliant minds have applied concentration, contemplation, and penetrating insight to the laws of physical nature, we can, for example, see and talk to people almost anywhere in the world through a hand-held electronic device. An occult power? Only to someone who has never seen this technology. But in the end the *sūtras* are not about technology any more than they are about the paranormal. Their real purpose is enlightenment and liberation.

3.17 **The arrangement [of the world of experience comes about] through the association, one with another, of word, meaning, and object. Analyzing them with total engagement [brings] knowledge of the all-pervading sound, [the syllable OM].**

शब्दार्थप्रत्ययानामितरेतराध्यासात्सङ्करस्-
तत्प्रविभागसंयमात्सर्वभूतरुतज्ञानम् ॥

śabdārthapratyayānām itaretarādhyāsāt saṅkaras
tatpravibhāgasaṁyamāt sarvabhūtarutajñānam

śabda: word
ārtha: meaning
pratyaya: idea, conception, anything present to awareness
itaretara: one another
adhyāsa: sitting upon, superimposing, layering
saṅkara: arrangement, mixing
tad: that (arrangement)
pravibhāga: separation, analysis
saṁyama: total mental engagement, full comprehension
sarvabhūta: everywhere existing, all-pervading, omnipresent
ruta: sound, roar, the call of an animal or bird; here, the praṇava
jñāna: knowledge

This highly technical *sūtra* is based on the idea of speech as creative power. To begin, let's return to the example of an apple. You see an apple. It may be something you want to eat. What if there is no apple present, but I say the word *apple?*

Because of the meaning it carries, the word alone may be enough to set your mouth watering and may even motivate you to go in search of an apple. By analyzing and understanding the differences of object, word, and meaning—all *effects* of the creation—we can gain knowledge of their ultimate *cause*.

The syllable OM represents the ultimate cause—the Supreme Being, one with its creative power. In the beginning, OM is the first sound heard to reverberate, and from it emerge all other sounds, the alphabet of creation. In *sūtra* 1.27 we learned that the vibration of OM embodies the divine presence, which *sūtra* 1.25 described as the source of all knowledge.

Creation through the Word is found in the Vedas and also in the ancient Hebrew, Greek, and Christian traditions. In the first chapter of Genesis the phrase "and God said" signals successive stages in the unfolding of the universe. For the ancient Greeks the Word (*logos*) signified the divine creative and controlling power in the cosmos. The opening of the Gospel of John also employs *logos*: "In the beginning was the Word, and the Word was with God, and the Word was God. ... All things were made by him ... ."

Vyāsa's commentary on the first part of this *sūtra* quotes the grammarian Patañjali (not the Patañjali of the *Yogasūtra*), who observed that when we hear the word *cow*, the image of the flesh-and-blood animal immediately comes to mind. We associate the string of sounds that make up the word with the physical cow and also with the idea of the cow. We fuse word, object, and idea together as if they were one. That is why the word *apple* can set your mouth watering, even though no physical apple is present. Life as we know it is based on the interaction of thought and matter.

After a detailed explanation, Vyāsa concludes his commentary by merely quoting the last clause, *sarvabhūtarutajñānam,* as if he doesn't know what to make of it. Vācaspati Miśra makes the astonishing declaration that it is "proven" that *saṁyama* on speech empowers a *yogin* to understand every human language as well as the sounds of animals and all other living creatures! That has been the accepted interpretation ever since, but is it correct?

The compound *sarvabhūtarutajñānam* is traditionally read as *sarvabhūtāṇāṁ rutasya jñānam,* "knowledge of the sounds of all creatures." This does not fit logically with what has gone before.

Why would complete insight into the relationship of word, meaning, and object in highly developed human speech lead to knowledge of the rudimentary roars and chirps and hums of animals, birds, and insects? It's like saying that by mastering calculus you can learn how to add, subtract, multiply, and divide!

A better way to interpret this is to take the words in their most basic sense. The adjective *sarvabhūta* means "existing everywhere"; it modifies *ruta,* which means "sound." (Secondarily *ruta* denotes a panoply of specific animal, bird, and insect calls.) At its simplest, *sarvabhūtarutajñānam* means "knowledge of the sound existing everywhere."

And what is that? It is OM. The technical term for OM is *praṇava,* which in its basic sense means "sound," "roar," "bellow," or "reverberation." Clearly *ruta* is a metaphor for the *praṇava,* the primordial vibration of divine consciousness, the source of creation.

3.18 **Knowledge of previous births [comes about] through perceiving the [mind's] latent impressions directly.**

संस्कारसाक्षात्करणात् पूर्वजातिज्ञानम् ॥

saṁskārasākṣātkaraṇāt pūrvajātijñānam

saṁskāra: latent mental impression
sākṣāt: with one's own eyes, clearly, visibly, actually, directly
karaṇa: making, effecting
pūrva: former, previous
jāti: birth
jñāna: knowledge

The present is the product of the past, and the future will be the outcome of the present. How does this universal principle apply to us as individuals? We are, at any moment, the sum total of our past experience. By looking deep inside ourselves, we discover how we came to be who and what we are.

The soul remains caught up in the natural cycle of cause and effect until liberated. As long as it remains bound, which is to say unenlightened, cause and effect will perpetuate the round of birth, life, death, and rebirth, lifetime after lifetime.

3.19 **Through [full comprehension] of the contents of one's own mind [arises] knowledge of the minds of others.**

प्रत्ययस्य परचित्तज्ञानम् ॥

pratyayasya paracittajñānam

pratyaya: idea, conception, anything present to awareness
para: other
citta: mind, the individual's field of awareness
jñāna: knowledge

Once we have explored our own subconscious and brought the buried impressions to the surface, our expanded awareness of ourselves allows us to understand the mental processes of others. We become good judges of character, able to observe others closely and to know "what makes them tick."

Although Patañjali doesn't point it out, this works both ways. As we observe others, we discover that their behavior can also shed light on our own, serving as a mirror in which to view ourselves. At the same time, I have a unique personality and so do you, because every personality is made up of a different selection from the same stock of elements. That's why every person is unique—and also so very similar, sharing the same humanity.

3.20 **But *not* of the content of another's mind, since that is not the object [of one's own] mind.**

न च तत्सालम्बनं तस्याविषयीभूतत्वात् ॥

na ca tat sālambanaṁ tasyāviṣayībhūtatvāt

na: not
ca: and
tad: that (knowledge)
sa: with
ālambana: the connection between a thought and its underlying cause (the mental impression)
tasya: its
aviṣayībhūtatva: the state of not being the object

Yes, we can know what makes a person tick, but we cannot expect literal access to someone else's thoughts. That would involve making the content of our own mind identical to someone else's. Patañjali wants to make it clear that having insight into a person's character is *not* mind-reading.

3.21 **Through full comprehension of the nature of the manifest world and suppression of the ability to perceive it by [mentally] disconnecting the eye from the light, [the manifest universe] vanishes [from awareness].**

कायरूपसंयमात्तद्ग्राह्यशक्तिस्तम्भे
चक्षुःप्रकाशासम्प्रयोगेऽन्तर्धानम् ॥

kāyarūpasaṁyamāt tadgrāhyaśaktistambhe
cakṣuḥprakāśāsamprayoge 'ntardhānam

kāya: body, assemblage, multitude; here, the manifest world
rūpa: nature, character
saṁyama: total mental engagement, full comprehension
tad: it (the body or the universe)
grāhya: to be perceived
śakti: power, ability
stambha: stoppage, obstruction, suppression
cakṣus: the faculty of seeing, sight, the eye
prakāśa: light, radiance
asamprayoga: disjoining, disconnection
antardhāna: disappearance, invisibility

Blocking the flow of light to the eyes makes the physical world disappear, but merely closing the eyes is not an advanced yogic discipline. Patañjali is talking about a metaphorical closure. In the Śaiva tradition when Śiva, the supreme consciousness, "opens his eyes," cosmic manifestation results. When he "closes his eyes," it goes away, and he rests in his eternally changeless being. We must go well beyond the mere physical closing of the eyes and cultivate a higher level of consciousness utterly detached from the external world.

The traditional reading is different. The classical commentators hold that "by fully understanding the body's nature and suppressing the ability to perceive it through the disconnection of the eye and the light, invisibility [results]." According to them, a *yogin* can become invisible by obstructing the light waves that travel to another's eyes.

In 2013 George Eleftheriades and Michael Selvanayagam published a paper in the journal *Physical Review X* on their experiment in "active electromagnetic cloaking." They surrounded an object with small antennas that radiated an electromagnetic field to cancel the radio waves that the object would naturally reflect. With the "cloak" in place, the object was undetectable to radar. Some day, the researchers predicted, the technology will extend to light waves as well, producing physical invisibility. The principle is just as Patañjali's commentators understood, but its implementation is through physical science, not meditation.

3.22 **Karma is [either] set in motion or not [yet] set in motion. Full comprehension of it [reveals] knowledge of its ultimate end—indeed according to the signs.**

सोपक्रमं निरुपक्रमं च कर्म
तत्संयमादपरान्तज्ञानमरिष्टेभ्यो वा ॥

sopakramaṁ nirupakramaṁ ca karma tatsaṁyamād aparāntajñānam ariṣṭebhyo vā

sopakrama: set about, undertaken, commenced
nirupakrama: not set about, not yet undertaken, not yet commenced
ca: and, or
karma: action, the accumulated effects of past deeds and their consequences
tad: it (karma)
saṁyama: total mental engagement, full comprehension
apara: having nothing beyond, ultimate
anta: end, outcome
jñāna: knowledge
ariṣṭa: sign, portent, omen, misfortune, good fortune
vā: or, and, also, even, indeed

The word *karma* means "act" or "action." It refers to physical actions as well as mental ones—to anything that we do or think. It also signifies the results of those actions, indeed the sum total of all actions and their consequences. Karma is both about what we do and about what happens to us as a result.

The workings of karma are enormously complex. Some actions produce immediate results and others take a long while before their consequences become apparent, maybe stretching even beyond the boundaries of a single lifetime. At any time some of a person's karma has been set in motion while some lies dormant.

How it will all play out can be known only through extraordinary insight as the boundaries of understanding expand. Yet Patañjali is quick to note that there is nothing occult about this. After all, the focus of our heroic mental endeavor here is the principle of cause and effect itself! *Sūtra* 3.16 taught that by fully knowing and understanding the present, we can deduce facts about the past and future. Now again Patañjali shows that intense concentration can be an enhanced process of inference—our knowledge comes "indeed according to the signs," as he says.

The classical commentators, following Vyāsa, understand *aparāntajñāna* as "knowledge of death," but that does not mesh with the rest of the *sūtra*. Why would knowledge gained through a full understanding of universal causality be focused on the single and inevitable event of death? As with *sūtra* 3.17, taking the words in their basic sense produces a more satisfactory reading. *Aparajñāna* basically means "ultimate end." Granted, by lexical extension it can mean "death," but there is a complication. In the Hindu view death is *not* the ultimate end; but only one phase in the ever-repeating cycle of birth, life, death, and rebirth. The "ultimate end" here points to karma—and to the ultimate outcome of anything set into motion. As for the word *ariṣṭa,* the classical commentators all speak of "portents of death," but *ariṣṭa* means *any* sign, associated with either good fortune or misfortune. Karma is, at heart, a moral principle: good actions yield favorable results, and evil actions accordingly come to no good end.

3.23 **In [the full comprehension of] kindness [toward the fortunate, compassion for the distressed, delight in the virtuous, and equanimity toward the unvirtuous, one acquires specific] strengths.**

मैत्र्यादिषु बलानि ॥

maitryādiṣu balāni

maitri: friendliness, friendship, kindness
ādi: and the rest, and the like, and so on
bala: power, strength, might, force, vigor

Back in the first chapter, in *sūtra* 1.33, Patañjali advised nurturing certain attitudes and behaviors towards others for the sake of our own peace of mind. Here he returns to those same practices but now at a more elevated level—one that brings about a fundamental transformation in our own character. Obeying an ethical principle is one thing; fully understanding it brings an unprecedented level of mastery—the kind we see in those whom we call saints or great souls. Their influence long outlasts them.

3.24 **[With full comprehension] of [various] strengths [come] the strength of an elephant, and so on.**

बलेषु हस्तिबलादीनि ॥

baleṣu hastibalādīni

bala: power, strength, might, force, vigor
hastin: elephant
bala: power, strength, might, force, vigor
ādi: and the rest, and the like, and so on

This *sūtra* is not meant to be taken literally. In *sūtra* 1.41 Patañjali noted that the mind becomes "colored" by the properties of an object present to it, just as a transparent crystal reflects the color of anything nearby. The example illustrated the process of ordinary perception. Now Patañjali takes that principle to a higher level. Instead of mere, passing coloration, we have identification. The message is, "As you think, so you become"—a universal spiritual truth.

3.25 **Fixing the perception outwardly [brings] knowledge of the subtle, the veiled, and the distant.**

प्रवृत्त्यालोकन्यासात्सूक्ष्मव्यवहितविप्रकृष्टज्ञानम् ॥

pravṛttyālokanyāsāt sūkṣmavyavahitaviprakṛṣṭajñānam

pravṛtti: outward motion of the mind
āloka: seeing, perception
nyāsa: setiing down, placing, fixing
sūkṣma: subtle
vyavahita: covered, concealed, not immediately connected
viprakṛṣṭa: distant, remote
jñāna: knowledge

An acutely heightened discipline of inner focus, when once again turned outward, produces enhanced powers of perception. Seeing "the subtle" means being able to notice objects or to grasp ideas that others overlook. "The veiled" refers to what is already there, just awaiting disclosure. We all have our "it's-as-plain-as-the-nose-on-your-face" moments when our awareness is acute. "The distant" refers to insights that may seem well out of range but, with our heightened abilities, suddenly appear in a spontaneous flash of understanding.

3.26 **Through total engagement with the sun [arises] knowledge of everything in the universe.**

भुवनज्ञानं सूर्ये संयमात् ॥

bhuvanajñānaṁ sūrye saṁyamāt

bhuvana: the world, the full extent of creation
jñāna: knowledge
sūrya: sun
saṁyama: total mental engagement, full comprehension

This and the next two *sūtras* evoke the sun, the moon, and the polestar as distant objects in the physical universe, but they are meant here in a symbolic sense. The sun represents the illuminating power by which all things are known. Just as the sun in the sky shines forth and makes visible everything in the world, so does the light of consciousness shine forth and bring everything to our awareness—even our very existence! Behind "I am"—our most basic knowledge—is the light of the Self.

3.27 **Through the moon, knowledge of the stars' arrangement.**

चन्द्रे ताराव्यूहज्ञानम् ॥

candre tārāvyūhajñānam

candra: moon
tārā: star
vyūha: position, arrangement, orderly arrangement of the parts of a whole
jñāna: knowledge

The moon is a metaphor for the known object. By understanding the nature of the object, we understand the nature of everything in the creation—symbolized by the stars that fill the heavens. Their arrangement signifies cosmic order.

3.28 **Through the polestar, knowledge of the stars' motion.**

ध्रुवे तद्गतिज्ञानम् ॥

dhruve tadgatijñānam

dhruva: the polestar
tad: of them (the stars)
gati: motion, movement
jñāna: knowledge

Once we fully understand how every material and mental principle has a place in the world, we can go on to look at how they all work. Everything is relative, and the polestar symbolizes the necessary, unmoving point of reference by which one thing makes sense in light of another.

This principle of a fixed point of orientation was well known to ancient navigators, who used the invariable position of the polestar to determine direction and latitude. Because that knowledge empowered them to travel the seas, the polestar is an apt metaphor for a mental orientation designed to help us navigate the ocean of existence—another common Hindu metaphor.

3.29 **Through the navel, knowledge of the body's structure.**

नाभिचक्रे कायव्यूहज्ञानम् ॥

nābhicakre kāyavyūhajñānam

nābhi: navel
cakra: wheel, circle, astronomical circle
kāya: body
vyūha: orderly arrangement of the parts of a whole, structure
jñāna: knowledge

The last three *sūtras* dealt with insights derived from contemplating the macrocosm "out there." This one and the two that follow will deal with the microcosm, using the symbolism of something close at hand—the human body.

Like the polestar, the navel symbolizes the principle of having a frame of reference. We need a perspective on our existence as flesh-and-blood creatures in order to gain complete insight into the nature of our human embodiment.

3.30 **Through the pit of the throat, the cessation of hunger and thirst.**

कण्ठकूपे क्षुत्पिपासानिवृत्तिः ॥

kaṇṭhakūpe kṣutpipāsānivṛttiḥ

kaṇṭha: throat

kūpa: pit, hollow
kṣut: hunger
pipāsā: thirst
nivṛtti: cessation, turning away, suspension, disappearance

Food and drink are, of course, physical necessities on which life depends, but their place in our lives can also be exaggerated until they become an overriding concern. There is wisdom in subduing the impulses of hunger and thirst.

A higher understanding of this *sūtra* rests on the common metaphor in Hindu teaching that food is anything taken in through the five senses. Just as we can be enslaved by the cravings of the stomach, we can be enslaved by the cravings of the mind. The words *hunger* and *thirst* are traditional metaphors for *desire*. Ask yourself, is it better to fulfill a thousand desires or to conquer one?

3.31 **Through the "tortoise shell," steadiness.**

कूर्मनाड्यां स्थैर्यम् ॥

kūrmanāḍyāṁ sthairyam

kūrma: tortoise
nāḍī: tube, hollow enclosure; here, by extension, a shell
sthairya: steadiness, stability, immobility, calmness, tranquility

This colorful metaphor grabs our attention and drives home the point. Just as the tortoise withdraws its limbs and head into its shell, remaining immobile and detached from the outer world, so should the spiritual aspirant withdraw the senses from their objects. As we already know, that withdrawal (the fifth limb of yoga) confers mastery over the senses.

Now Patañjali takes the teaching to a higher level. Full comprehension of the "tortoise shell" is the ability to reverse the flow of consciousness—to turn it back upon itself so that it becomes the focus of its own contemplation. That leads to a hitherto unimagined steadiness of mind.

3.32 **Perfection is evident in the radiance of spiritual exaltation.**

मूर्धज्योतिषि सिद्धदर्षनम् ॥

mūrdhajyotiṣi siddhadarśanam

mūrdha: head, summit, state of spiritual exaltation
jyotis: light, radiance, shining
siddha: perfection, attainment
darśana: perception

Holy men and women—those among us who are in touch with their higher, divine nature—have a spiritual glow, an aura that others can sense. It's not a physical light, even though religious art depicts it as a halo surrounding the head.

We cannot recognize something in another if it is not present within ourselves. When realized, our own higher nature will shine forth. In the Chāndogyopaniṣad (4.9.1–3), when the teacher Gautama beheld the transformation in his disciple Satyakāma, he exclaimed, "You shine like a knower of Brahman."

3.33 **Indeed through [such] illumination [comes] knowledge of everything.**

प्रातिभाद्वा सर्वम् ॥

pratibhād vā sarvam

pratibha: splendor, light, intelligence, understanding, supreme consciousness, divine awareness
vā: or, and, also, even, indeed
sarva: all

Every tradition that recognizes divinity—either as the Supreme Being (God) or as supreme being (our own highest nature)—endows it with omniscience. When the limitations of human intelligence are removed, our awareness expands and rises to an all-knowing perspective (call it a "God's-eye view") in which the essence of everything is revealed.

3.34 **Awareness of the mind [resides] in the heart.**

हृदये चित्तसंवित् ॥

hṛdaye cittasaṁvit

hṛdaya: heart, center, essence
citta: mind, the individual's field of awareness
saṁvit: consciousness, awareness

The heart is a long-established metaphor for consciousness, the supreme reality, the Self, Brahman. The mind is the instrument of consciousness through which we experience our existence in this world. Being finite, the mind can only let us know finite things—all the diverse facets of the creation. It cannot bring us to the supreme knowledge, for that belongs to the heart alone.

3.35 **To experience the [outer] world is not to distinguish between the luminosity [of the mind] and consciousness itself, which are entirely distinct. Self-knowledge [arises] from fully Self-directed contemplation apart from any other intention.**

सत्त्वपुरुषयोरत्यन्तासङ्कीर्णयोः प्रत्ययाविशेषो भोगः
परार्थत्वात्स्वार्थसंयमात्पुरुषज्ञानम् ॥

sattvapuruṣayor atyantāsaṁkīrṇayoḥ pratyayāviśeṣo bhogaḥ parārthatvāt svārthasaṁyamāt puruṣajñānam

sattva: luminosity (of the mind)
puruṣa: consciousness, the Self
atyanta: complete, entire, unlimited
asaṁkīrṇa: unmixed, distinct
pratyaya: idea, conception, anything present to awareness
aviśeṣa: nondistinction
bhoga: experience of the manifest creation
parārthatva: the state of having something else as its object
svārtha: having itself as its object or purpose
saṁyama: total mental engagement, full comprehension
puruṣa: consciousness, the Self
jñāna: knowledge

This *sūtra* is an extended philosophical reflection on the difference between bondage and freedom. Worldly experience is a matter of intention or will, but Self-knowledge comes through a higher aspiration. The human condition depends on the reflected light of the mind, but Self-knowledge is the experience of the self-luminosity of consciousness itself. Enlightenment depends on discerning between the two, and Patañjali will revisit this theme in *sūtras* 3.49, 3.53, and 3.55.

3.36 **Accordingly, hearing, touch, vision, taste, smell, and awareness are born.**

ततः प्रातिभश्रावणवेदनादर्शास्वादवार्ता जायन्ते ॥

tataḥ prātibhaśrāvaṇavedanādarśāsvādavārtā jāyante

tatas: therefore, consequently, for that reason
prātibha: awareness
śrāvaṇa: hearing
vedanā: touching
ādarśa: seeing
āsvāda: tasting
vārta: smelling
jāyante: are born

All of our faculties of perception are conduits for knowledge of the world "out there." It is the working of the mind that makes sense of it all and transforms it into the multilayered richness of experience that we call human life. This extends all the way from sensory perception to the lofty level of intuitive insight.

3.37 **These are worldly accomplishments but obstacles to meditative union.**

ते समाधावुपसर्गा व्युत्थाने सिद्धयः ॥

te samādhāv upasargā vyutthāne siddhayaḥ

te: they
samādhi: meditative union, unitary consciousness

upasarga: obstacle
vyutthāna: the manifest or external world
siddhi: accomplishment, attaintment, perfection

To repeat: "To experience this [stilling of consciousness] is to abide in one's own essential nature. Otherwise one identifies with the mind's activities." All perceiving and thinking remain externally focused, for they all deal with the manifest world. They cannot lead to the experience of the true Self, which transcends the world.

From Vyāsa's time onward, commentators have understood *sūtras* 3.16–48 as detailing occult powers, but as we have seen so far, they can be interpreted metaphorically or abstractly as pointing to higher and simpler spiritual truths. Here it may serve well to recount an Indian fable:

One of two brothers went away to practice austerities; the other remained the village. After a few years the first returned, and the two went out for a walk. When they came to a river, the brother who had stayed in the village paid the ferryman and crossed the river, while the other, now an accomplished *yogin,* demonstrated his power to walk across the water. When they met up on the other side, the first brother observed, "So this is what you've gained from all your years of austerity—something worth no more than two cents!"

3.38 **Through relaxing the cause of bondage and perceiving its ways [comes] entry into other bodies.**

बन्धकारणशैथिल्यात्प्रचारसंवेदनाच्च चित्तस्य परशरीरावेशः ॥

bandhakāraṇaśaithilyāt pracārasaṁvedanāc ca cittasya paraśarīrāveśaḥ

bandha: bondage
kāraṇa: effecting
śaithilya: relaxation, diminution, inattention
pracāra: way, custom, habit, usage

saṁvedana: the act of perceiving or feeling, perception
ca: and
citta: mind, the individual's field of awareness
para: other
śarīra: body, any solid body
āveśa: joining oneself, entry, entrance

When you understand the essence of your own human embodiment apart from and underlying all your diverse experiences, you understand that same essence in everything. That is what is meant by entering into the bodies of others. This *sūtra* is not a statement of occult power but of genuine mystical experience. Going well beyond the empathy suggested in *sūtra* 3.19, it takes our awareness beyond the confines of our own ego-self to the experience of a vibrant, all-unifying selfhood.

The Sanskrit language even has a word for this. *Sarvātmabhāva* is the experience of expanded consciousness in which the sense of self, once confined to one's own body, is felt to fill the whole of creation. The sky, the sun, the earth, the trees, indeed *everything* is alive with selfhood, and that selfhood is One. The Bhagavadgītā (6.29) expresses this beautifully:

> One who is established in yoga beholds the vision of
> sameness everywhere,
> the Self present in all beings and all beings in the Self.

3.39 **Through a joyous spirit one wins detachment from water, mud, thorns, and [all] the rest, and they go away.**

उदानजयाज्जलपङ्ककण्टकादिष्वसङ्ग उत्क्रान्तिश् च ॥

udānajayāj jalapaṅkakaṇṭakādiṣv asaṅga utkrāntiś ca

udāna: breathing upwards; in Buddhism, joy
jaya: mastery
jala: water
paṅka: mud
kaṇṭaka: thorn, pointed object, sting, any source of annoyance
ādi: and the rest, and the like, and so on

asaṅga: nonattachment, disinclination
utkrānti: passing away, going out, dying
ca: and

Sitting suspended in mid air, walking on water, or resting comfortably on a bed of nails—those are images of the yogi in the popular imagination, and that is how this *sūtra* is traditionally understood. All of those powers have to do with overcoming gravity. But what does that have to do with inner peace?

Patañjali, once again, is speaking in metaphors. This *sūtra* is not about levitation. It is about rising above the difficulties of human life—about having a buoyant spirit, about not being drowned in despair, about not being mired in a sense of helpless limitation, about being immune to life's stings. Through seeing the divine in and through all things, we gain a joyful attitude. And, yes, in that joy we rise above the fray.

3.40 **Through winning [the vision of] the universal [comes] illumination.**

समानजयाज्ज्वलनम् ॥

samānajayāt jvalanam

samāna: same, equal, universal
jaya: mastery, victory, winning
jvalana: radiance, illumination

Having attained the experience of universal selfhood, we perceive everything in the light of right understanding. It's not a matter of seeing different things but of seeing things differently—in the light of a higher, unifying awareness.

This *sūtra* is unusually obscure, but its sense follows in the context of the preceding one. The classical commentators are often bent on literal readings and occult powers, but here Vyāsa limits himself to a single comment: "One who obtains mastery over the *samāna* [the vital breath responsible for the digestion of food], blows the fire into flame and thus shines." The normally verbose Vācaspati Miśra does no better with his *two* sentences: "Fire is of the body. 'Blowing it into flame' means rendering it brighter." Not knowing what to say, they show more discretion than Vijñānabhiksu, who sees here the yogic power of self-combustion!

3.41 **By fully comprehending the connection between space and hearing, "divine hearing" [results].**

श्रोत्राकाशयोः सम्बन्धसंयमाद्दिव्यं श्रोत्रम् ॥

śrotrākāśayoḥ sambandhasaṁyamād divyaṁ śrotram

śrotra: hearing
ākāśa: space (the subtlest of the five physical elements)
sambandha: connection, binding with, relationship
saṁyama: total mental engagement, full comprehension
divya: divine
śrotra: hearing

Someone says something to you, but you don't hear because your attention is engaged elsewhere. Your mind's activity drowns out the person's speech, and he or she may have to shout to be heard, when ordinarily a normal conversational tone would do. On the other hand, someone who has your full attention can speak in a whisper and you will hear.

This *sūtra* alludes to the connection between space and hearing as explained in the Sāṁkhya philosophy's blueprint of the universe. Space is the medium through which sound travels, and hearing is our capacity to receive the sound. But we still have to know how to make the connection, how to "tune in." By directing attention to the way we hear, we naturally become more attentive.

How attentive can we become? We've all heard the expression "still, small voice." Quieter than a whisper, it comes not from "out there" but from within. We hear it not with the physical ears but with "divine hearing." In the stillness of intense contemplation we become receptive to the voice of our own higher Self. We tune in to a subtler level beyond the range of physical sound. It is in this intimate communication that we "hear" profound spiritual truths and are granted life-changing insights that would not have occurred to us otherwise. These revelations demonstrate that the answers to life's deepest questions come not from a divine being "out there" but from one deep within.

Interestingly, Vyāsa merely observes that the power of hearing is the means of perceiving sound, provided that no obstruction should intervene in space. Vācaspati Miśra writes at length, almost scientifically, about the nature and processes of sense perception. Neither commentator attempts to explain "divine hearing" in terms of the occult.

3.42 **By fully comprehending the connection between the body and space and by identifying with the unimpeded air, motion through the space [of consciousness results].**

कायाकाशयोः सम्बन्धसंयमाल्लघु-
तूलसमापत्तेश्चाकाशगमनम् ॥

kāyākāśayoḥ sambandhasaṁyamāl laghutūlasamāpatteś cākāśagamanam

kāya: body
ākāśa: space
sambandha: connection, binding together, relationship
saṁyama: total mental engagement, full comprehension
laghu: light, swift, nimble, agile, unimpeded
tūla: air, atmosphere, sky, cotton
samāpatti: coming together, convergence, attaining to
ca: and
ākāśa: space
gamana: going, motion

The body has a relationship with the extremely subtle element of space. It occupies a certain volume and is restricted to one place at any given time. Every motion, no matter how small, even the blinking of an eye, involves an interaction of a physical form with the space that contains it. But how ephemeral the connection is! The movements leave absolutely no trace on the space just occupied.

Patañjali urges that we engage mentally with the air—the next subtlest element after space—which is light, swift, agile, and unimpeded. As you think, so you become. We can break the identification with the body and go beyond our earth-bound condition to an expanded sense of selfhood.

3.43 **This experience of the mind outside [the body] is not imagined; it is an incorporeal [state] of elevated awareness. Because of it the veil that conceals the light of the Self wears away.**

बहिरकल्पिता वृत्तिर्महाविदेहा ततः

प्रकाशावरणक्षयः ॥

bahirakalpitā vṛttir mahāvidehā tataḥ
prakāśāvaraṇakṣayaḥ

bahis: external
akalpita: not imagined
vṛtti: activity or modification of the mind
mahat: great; in Sāṁkhya, the buddhi, the highest level of human intelligence
videha: incorporeal, disembodied, disincarnate
tatas: from that
prakāśa: shining forth of consciousness
āvaraṇa: veiling
kṣaya: waning, dwindling, diminution, wasting away, destruction

We can easily project ourselves outward by thinking that we are here or there, doing this or that. It's called daydreaming, but the state of consciousness described here is not the product of imagination. It is the experience of the uppermost region of the human mind apart from any identification with the body. This physically borderless state lies far along the way to true Self-knowledge.

3.44 **Victory over the manifest world [comes about] through total engagement with the nature of the tangible, its natural connection with the intangible and the meaning [of it all].**

स्थूलस्वरूपसूक्ष्मान्वयार्थवत्त्वसंयमाद्भूतजयः ॥

sthūlasvarūpasūkṣmānvayārthavattvasaṁyamād bhūtajayaḥ

sthūla: gross, tangible, material, dense
svarūpa: essential nature, essence
sūkṣma: fine, subtle, intangible
anvaya: connection, succession, natural order
arthavattva: significance
saṁyama: total mental engagement, full comprehension
bhūta: that which exists, the world
jaya: mastery

The previous *sūtra* taught that mental disengagement from the physical body points to the nature of the Self as the pure radiance of consciousness. However, the goal still lies ahead. The mind may no longer be tied to the body, and the sense of self may now be felt to pervade the universe, as described in *sūtra* 3.38, but the universe is still present to that mind. Only through full knowledge of everything in the universe and of how it all works can we break its hold. This does not mean learning every fact about every thing—that is impossible. It does mean that we cannot transcend our finite existence until we know just what it is that we are trying to transcend.

The evolution of the cosmos flows from the most subtle (*sūkṣma*) principle, which is the highest aspect of human consciousness (*buddhi* or *mahat*), all the way down to the most dense (*sthūla*), which is "earth," meaning solid physical matter. Along the way each principle (*tattva*) interacts with the others to produce the world we know. This world, for us, exists only in our experience of it, and knowing how it comes about is the key to freedom. This *sūtra* is a clear reference to the Sāṁkhya blueprint of creation, which will be outlined in the commentary on *sūtra* 3.47.

3.45 **With this [mastery], as such subtler states manifest, [one is] no longer assailed by having a body and all that comes with it.**

ततोऽणिमादिप्रादुर्भावः कायसम्पत्तद्धर्मानभिघातश्च ॥

tataḥ 'ṇimādiprādurbhāvaḥ kāyasampattad-dharmānabhighātaś ca

tatas: from that
aṇiman: subtle state, minuteness (of an atom)
ādi: such as, and the rest, and the like, and so on
prādurbhāva: manifestation
kāya: body
sampat: being possessed of, the state of having
tad: that (having a body)
dharma: that which is according to the nature of something
anabhighāta: unassailed
ca: and

Through higher spiritual understanding, we become impervious to the usual discomforts of life. Even so, as long as a person self-identifies even slightly as a body-mind complex, he or she has to relate to an external world. That is why the practice of yoga is about turning attention away from the outer and inward to the ever-perfect Self.

Commentators take the phrase *aṇimādi* (translated here as "such subtler states") in the esoteric sense of the eight occult powers enumerated in classic Hindu texts, often in mythological or hagiographic narratives. *Aṇiman* is the ability to become as small as an atom; *mahiman*, to make the body as large or heavy as desired; *laghiman*, to make the body weightless; *prāpti*, to do anything however impossible it may seem; *prākāmya*, to have nothing stand in one's way; *vāśitva*, to control the elements and other living beings; *īśitṛtvā*, to manifest objects; and *yatrakāmavasāyitva*, to fulfill any wish.

Patañjali does not enumerate these eight occult powers, much less comment on them. Moreover the basic sense of *aṇimādi* as "such subtler states"—those described in the previous fourteen *sūtras*—fits his context.

3.46 **The possession of a body [is what stands] amid the complexities of appearance, personality, ability, and endurance.**

रूपलावण्यबलवज्रसंहननत्वानि कायसम्पत् ॥

rūpalāvaṇyabalavajrasaṁhananatvāni kāyasampat

rūpa: beauty, appearance, form
lāvaṇya: charm, loveliness
bala: power, strength, might, vigor
vajra: adamant (an unyieldingly hard substance), endurance
saṁhananatva: combination, conjunction, complexity
kāya: body
sampat: being possessed of, the state of having

Why does Patañjali now turn our attention back to the body? In spite of the dawning intimations of our true nature, these are still only brief flashes. We still have to deal with the deeply ingrained tendencies that come with thinking of ourselves as body-mind creatures. We may now have good meditations, a higher understanding of life, even glimpses of divinity, but we are not yet free of the underlying patterns of being human.

How do I look? Am I handsome or beautiful? Can I improve my appearance? How do I behave? Am I pleasant or charming? What am I capable of? Am I physically strong or do my strengths lie in abilities of another kind? And do I have the power to endure all of life's ups and downs? All the thoughts that come to us so casually and unremittingly in the course of an ordinary day remain as obstacles to be overcome.

3.47 **Through total engagement with the significance of how the ego's own nature and its perceptions connect, mastery over the senses [comes about].**

ग्रहणस्वरूपास्मितान्वयार्थवत्त्वसंयमाद् इन्द्रियजयः ॥

grahaṇasvarūpāsmitānvayārthavattvasaṁyamād indriyajayaḥ

grahaṇa: grasping, perception
svarūpa: essential nature
asmitā: ego, egoity
anvaya: natural order, causal connection
arthavattva: significance, meaning
saṁyama: total mental engagement, full comprehension
indriya: faculty of perception, sense
jaya: mastery

Why is all that preoccupation with the mundane so hard to overcome? In a word, the ego. Everything we know is colored by our own particular point of view. I am a unique individual, at the very center of all that I perceive. What the ego perceives it also grasps, it makes its own. I know what I like, I know what I don't like, and I have strong feelings about many things. In a word, I react. What I fail to understand is that being reactive means not being in control, even though I find myself always at the center of my experience. I need to understand why.

It is not enough to know that there is a connection. We need to know the *significance* of the connection—that we create our own bondage and that we can do something about it. *Sūtra* 2.55 spoke of mastery over the operation of the senses through the withdrawal of the mind. That was breaking the outer connection. Here Patañjali shows how to break the inner link.

Knowing exactly what everything in the universe is, how it is all connected, and how it functions is essential to spiritual mastery. This is where the Sāṁkhya blueprint of creation comes in. (It is such an effective paradigm that it was adopted with minor modifications by other schools of Indian thought, such as the Vedānta and the Tantric Śaiva lineages.) According to the Sāṁkhya scheme, there are twenty-five cosmic principles. *Puruṣa* is the self-aware subject. *Prakṛti* is the potential source of the objective universe. These two are eternal. Within *prakṛti* the remaining twenty-three principles produce the ever-changing world we know. The highest principle within *prakṛti* is *buddhi* or *mahat*, the determinative capacity of intelligence. From that evolves *asmitā*, the principle of ego, more often called *ahaṁkāra*, the "I-maker." From *ahaṁkāra* evolves *manas*, the cognitive function that receives and processes sensory data. The remaining principles are the five sensory faculties, the five motor capacities, the five subtle elements (the sensory stimuli), and the five principles of physicality, known as the gross elements.

3.48 **From that [arises] swiftness of mind, a state free from the senses, and mastery over the origin of the manifest universe.**

ततो मनोजवितम्विकरणभावः प्रधानजयश्च ॥

tato manojavitvam vikaraṇabhāvaḥ pradhānajayaś ca

tatas: from that
manas: mind
javitva: swiftness, fleetness
vikaraṇa: without instruments (the five faculties of perception)
bhāva: state, condition
pradhāna: origin or source of the manifest universe
jaya: mastery
ca: and

Ordinary knowledge—which means our everyday experience of life in this world—comes through some medium. Perceptions flow in through the instruments of the five senses. The instrument that is the mind processes them as perceptual knowledge and may create the next higher level of conceptual knowledge by forming abstract ideas. Both levels are called mediate knowledge, because the knowledge is not direct but comes about through an instrument.

Above them lies the level of intuitive knowledge, which is immediate, meaning direct. Here awareness bypasses the processes of the perceiving and thinking mind and goes right to the source. "Swiftness of mind" means intuition that comes in a flash, without having to think anything through. This spontaneous kind of knowing reveals the true essence of everything. Once we fully understand, the spell is broken, and with it the hold of mundane existence.

3.49 **Omniscience and supremacy over all existence [belong] only to one who discerns the difference between the highest human intelligence and the [supreme] Self.**

सत्त्वपुरुषान्यताख्यातिमात्रस्य सर्वभावाधिष्ठातृत्वं सर्वज्ञात्त्वम् च ॥

sattvapuruṣānyatākhyātimātrasya
sarvabhāvādhiṣṭhātṛtvam sarvajñātṛtvam ca

sattva: the highest aspect of human intelligence, buddhi
puruṣa: the Self as pure consciousness
anyatā: difference, otherness
khyāti: discernment
mātra: only
sarva: all
bhāva: state of existence
adhiṣṭhātṛtva: supremacy
sarvajñātṛtva: omniscience
ca: and

Omniscience and supremacy are attributes of the Divine. They mean infinite knowledge and infinite power. Human knowledge and human power are, by their very nature, limited. It follows that the difference between the human condition and true Self-knowledge is the difference between experiencing oneself as finite or infinite.

The self-aware Self abides apart from anything of an objective nature that can limit or define it. Recall *sūtra* 1.3: "To experience this is to abide in one's own essential nature." In contrast, the ego-self associates with any number of finite objects, physical and mental, and declares, "This is who I am." As Patañjali expressed it in *sūtra* 1.4: "Otherwise one identifies with the mind's activities." No amount of finite qualities adds up to the infinite. To be infinite is to be free of the finite.

In the end it all comes down to a simple distinction of subject and object, but at a level of subtlety well beyond that of ordinary human awareness. The Self is the ultimate subject; by its light and its light alone is anything of an objective nature known. Which is my true identity? The self-luminous Self, all-knowing and all-powerful—which is to say divine—or that same light of awareness, reflected and diminished to a sense of small and imperfect identity that came about through a faulty association with the mind's activities?

3.50 **Out of dispassion toward even that [omniscience and supremacy], with the fading away of [even] potential faults, [comes] liberation.**

तद्वैराग्यादपि दोषबीजक्षये कैवल्यम् ॥

tad vairāgyād api doṣabījakṣaye kaivalyam

tad: that (divine omniscience and supremacy)
vairāgya: dispassion, detachment
api: even
doṣa: fault, defect
bīja: seed
kṣaya: waning, dwindling, diminution, wasting away, destruction
kaivalya: aloneness, perfect isolation of consciousness from matter (Sāṁkhya definition); absolute unity, singularity (Advaita Vedānta definition)

In the inkling of an immeasurably grander Selfhood, the ego-self may be tempted to want to identify with its divine power and glory, claiming it for itself. That would only reinforce the binding sense of separate identity: "Look at how grand *I* am!" Here, as at every previous level of awakening, the need for dispassion and detachment continues. The next *sūtra* comes as a warning.

3.51 **Should the temptation of self-aggrandizement arise, no pride of attachment should be allowed, lest unwanted inclinations return.**

स्थान्युपनिमन्त्रणे सङ्गस्मयाकरणं पुनरनिष्टप्रसङ्गात् ॥

sthānyupanimantraṇe saṅgasmayākaraṇaṁ punaraniṣṭaprasaṅgāt

sthānin: occupying a high position
upanimantraṇa: invitation
saṅga: attachment, contact, association
smaya: smile, wonder, astonishment, conceit, pride
akaraṇa: absence of action
punar: again
aniṣṭa: undesired
prasaṅga: inclination

Overcoming one obstacle at a time, we have progressed from the journey's beginning to a place near the destination. However, old tendencies linger on in the form of subtle impressions, and backsliding is always a possibility. An advanced practitioner is still vulnerable, and as a familiar saying warns, "The bigger they are, the harder they fall."

3.52 **Through complete engagement with the moment and its succession [arises] knowledge born of discernment.**

क्षणतत्क्रमयोः संयमाद्विवेकजं ज्ञानम् ॥

kṣaṇatatkramayoḥ saṁyamād vivekajaṁ jñānam

kṣaṇa: moment, instant
tad: it
krama: sequence, succession
saṁyama: total mental engagement, full comprehension
viveka: discernment, discrimination
ja: born
jñāna: knowledge

Patañjali is telling us to be ever alert. Being "in the moment" has become a popular expression, but its casual use does not begin to reveal what it really means.

The "knowledge born of discernment" is Self-knowledge or enlightenment. How do we get there? The mind is in constant motion, with one thought following another in an endless flow. Each thought has a point of arising, a duration in time, and a point where it disappears. One after another, instant by instant, thoughts come, stay awhile, and go in an endless sequence. By recognizing the sequence, it is possible to focus attention on the point between the vanishing of one thought and the arising of the next. This point between thoughts is the moment. It is the point where there is no thought, no mental activity. It is the still ground. Focusing there brings about the stillness that Patañjali first mentioned in *sūtra* 1.2: "Yoga is the stilling of the mind's activity." That stilling is Self-knowledge, enlightenment, liberation.

3.53 **From that [degree of engagement one can] distinguish [between] two like objects that appear identical even in regard to position, characteristic, and category.**

जातिलक्षणदेशैरन्यताऽनवच्छेदात्तुल्ययोस्ततः प्रतिपत्तिः ॥

jātilakṣaṇadeśair anyatā 'navacchedāt tulyayos tataḥ pratipattiḥ

jāti: species, category, type
lakṣaṇa: distinguishing characteristic
deśa: place, spot, point, position
anyatā: difference, otherness
anavaccheda: nonseparation, nondistinction, nondiscrimination
tulya: similar, alike
tatas: from that, therefore
pratipatti: gaining, obtaining, perception, observation, ascertainment

To understand this *sūtra,* let's suppose there are three apples on a table. Looking at them, we know they are all apples and not oranges. That activity of the mind is distinction by category. We notice that two of the apples are green and one is red. That is distinction by characteristic. You remove the red apple and now have two apparently identical green apples on the table. You note that one is on the left and the other on the right. That is distinction by position. You leave the room, and someone switches the two apples. You return and know that this happened, because your powers of observation have grown that acute.

Does Patañjali say we should strive for such extraordinary powers of perception? At this stage of spiritual awakening, what would be the purpose? What he is saying is that we need an even keener power of discernment than that of distinguishing between identical objects in order to distinguish between our own highest intelligence and divine consciousness, mentioned in the previous *sūtra*.

To make that point Patañjali resorts to hyperbole. The present *sūtra* should be understood as a grand overstatement just to impress on us how extraordinarily refined our discernment must become before we can make that final distinction between the highest knowable aspect of selfhood in this human condition and the supreme Self that is our true being.

The highest aspect of humanity and the subtlest of all the principles of creation is the *buddhi,* the determinative faculty of intelligence. However, it still belongs to the realm of material nature (*prakṛti*) and is, by nature, an object. We need to distinguish between the *buddhi* in its highest degree of purity and the higher Self (*puruṣa*), the pure subject, uncolored by even a trace of objectivity. Like the moon, which symbolizes objectivity, the *buddhi* does not shine by its own light; what we experience as the highest human intelligence is in truth the reflected light of the Self, which, like the sun, shines of its own accord. The final act of discernment is to distinguish the reflected light of the self from the inherent light of the Self.

3.54 **Knowledge born of discernment is liberating, encompassing everything everywhere and without sequence. So it is.**

तारकं सर्वविषयं सर्वथाविषयमक्रमं चेति विवेकजं ज्ञानम् ॥

tārakaṁ sarvaviṣayaṁ sarvathāviṣayam akramaṁ ceti vivekajaṁ jñānam

tāraka: liberating
sarva: all
viṣaya: sphere, domain, region
sarvathā: everywhere
viṣaya: sphere, domain, region
akrama: nonsequential
ca: and
iti: thus
viveka: discernment, discrimination
ja: born
jñāna: knowledge

In the knowledge born of extraordinary discernment there is neither I nor other, but a wholeness without difference; there is neither here nor there, but a consciousness beyond space and time. That alone is the knowledge that liberates.

3.55 **When the highest human intelligence and divine consciousness are identically pure, liberation results.**

सत्त्वपुरुषयोः शुद्धिसाम्ये कैवल्यमिति ॥

sattvapuruṣayoḥ śuddhisāmye kaivalyam iti

sattva: the highest aspect of human intelligence, buddhi
puruṣa: the Self as pure consciousness
śuddhi: purity
sāmya: sameness, equality, homogeneity, identity
kaivalya: aloneness, perfect isolation of consciousness from matter, absolute unity, singularity
iti: thus

Once the highest experience of human consciousness has become totally devoid of objective content and activity, it is seen to be identical with divine consciousness. To attain that ultimate stillness is to recognize one's own true nature as the supreme Self. That is liberation.

CHAPTER 4

4.1 **Accomplishments are the products of birth, nurturance, resolution, discipline, and meditative union.**

जन्मौषधिमन्त्रतपःसमाधिजाः सिद्धयः ॥

janmauṣadhimantratapaḥsamādhijāḥ siddhayaḥ

janma: birth
oṣadhi: plant, herb, medicinal plant; here, nurturance
mantra: resolution, plan, design
tapas: ardent discipline, religious austerity
samādhi: meditative union, unitary consciousness
ja: born, produced
siddhi: accomplishment, fulfillment, attainment, success

The first chapter, describing the mind and its workings, took us from normal, everyday experience through higher states of awareness all the way to the ultimate Self-realization. The second and third chapters together followed that same trajectory with emphasis on the methods of practice. Now, at the beginning of the fourth chapter, we return to the here and now and will advance to full enlightenment and liberation.

In this first *sūtra* Patañjali speaks, partly in symbolic language, of accomplishments—of who and what we are now, how we got that way, and where we may be headed. In whatever way we understand ourselves, our sense of identity rests on what we have accomplished or actualized in life. The conditions and circumstances in which we find ourselves are "born" —that is to say, they come about—in five basic ways. Patañjali lists them in their logical order.

First, we are all born with certain talents, abilities, and personal characteristics. They are the results of previous lifetimes in the ongoing chain of birth, life, death, and rebirth, driven by cause and effect. At any moment each of us is the sum total of a unique past; even at the moment of birth each of us is unique. From the first breath, each person is already an individual unlike any other.

Next, in regard to nurturance the word Patañjali uses is *plants*. This is not the first time he has used something from the natural world as a symbol of a higher principle. In the previous chapter he invoked the sun, the moon, and the polestar in a metaphorical sense. In the ancient Vedic hymns and the Upaniṣads the word for *plant* refers to all growing things in general or more specifically to health-promoting or healing herbs. We take it here in the sense of food that sustains and nourishes the life of the body. And then we recall that in Hindu teaching *food* itself is a metaphor for anything taken in mentally through the five senses. Throughout the course of life, all our experiences continue to shape who we are, what we can do, how we think, and so on. Life is a formative process. In modern language we might understand the two terms *birth* and *plants* as signifying nature and nurture.

These two principles apply to any human life. With the third term Patañjali introduces the idea of resolution, plan, or design—what we personally want and what we are willing to work for.

That requires discipline, the fourth item in the list. Patañjali has spoken of the need for such discipline several times already, and we have seen that in its highest sense discipline is an ardent enthusiasm that purifies by directing the mind to higher levels of consciousness.

Finally, there is the achievement born of meditative union. When Patañjali first spoke of meditative union in *sūtra* 1.20, we understood it as the level of complete and undeviating absorption that brings us close to the ultimate goal. Because it lies just before the state of supreme, liberating Self-awareness, even an instantaneous flash of unitary consciousness will validate and reinforce our resolve. The deeper and longer the experience, the more it will transform our character.

To sum up, we are formed by nature, nurture, our own intentions, our own committed strivings, and transformative experience. In the next five *sūtras* Patañjali will consider each of these in turn.

This reading of the *sūtra* is vastly different from the traditional one. Beginning with Vyāsa all commentators take the word *siddhi* in the specialized sense of occult or paranormal powers. These, they say, can be evident from birth (*janma*), having been attained in past lives, or they can be had through the use of consciousness-altering drugs (*oṣadhi*), magical incantations (*mantra*), physical austerities (*tapas*), or meditative union (*samādhi*). Occasionally the commentators back up their claims by citing examples from ancient myths, taking them as literally true.

The Sāṁkhya scholar J. W. Hauer found this *sūtra* so troublesome that he dismissed it as a later interpolation. Edwin F. Bryant (pages 406–407) accepts it as valid and details the commentators' views, but he seems to treat the *sūtra* almost as an afterthought to the preceding chapter. "By the way, folks, I almost forgot—." But is that how Patañjali would begin a new chapter? Certainly not! Our reading conforms to his established method. In this first *sūtra* he introduces five terms, and in the next five *sūtras* he will elaborate on them, one at a time, just as he has done before.

4.2 **Change from one condition to another [comes about] because of the abundance [of possibilities] in nature.**

जात्यन्तरपरिणामः प्रकृत्यापूरात् ॥

jātyantarapariṇāmaḥ prakṛtyāpūrāt

jāti: form of existence or position assigned by birth, rank, caste, family, or lineage
antara: other

pariṇāma: change, transformation
prakṛti: nature, the realm of material creation, the original source of the evolved universe
āpūra: abundance

As long as we live our human lives, caught up in the ongoing activities of the mind, we experience constant interaction not only with the external world that we know through the senses but also with the internal domain of personality—of who and what we think ourselves to be and how we feel at any time. Life is the experience of constant change, never the same from one moment to the next. If that is true of one human life, it is true of all, and the possibilities are beyond number.

4.3 **[Human] motives do not drive [the principle of change] but they do effect the flow of events, just as a farmer [does not create the life-force in the seed but does affect its growth by controlling the flow of water to the field].**

निमित्तमप्रयोजकंप्रकृतीनां वरणभेदस्तु ततः क्षेत्रवत् ॥

nimittam aprayojakaṁ prakṛtīṇāṁ varaṇabhedas tu tataḥ kṣetrikavat

nimitta: cause, motive, reason
aprayojaka: not causing or effecting
prakṛti: here, the flow of natural events and processes
varaṇa: rampart, earthen mound, enclosure
bheda: breaking open, bursting asunder, breach, partition
tu: but
tatas: therefore
kṣetrika: farmer
vat: like

This *sūtra* elaborates on the idea of plants and nurturance. A farmer must first have the resolve to plant a crop. Then he works at the cultivation of his field by managing the irrigation channels so that each kind of plant receives the amount of water it requires for proper growth. By intelligent management he will reap an optimum harvest. But there is another lesson as well: although the farmer can plant the seeds in the field, he cannot plant the life-force in the seeds. That is a power he does not have.

The field is a classic metaphor for the human mind, the individual's field of awareness. Just as a farmer decides to open one irrigation channel and not another, controlling the flow of water to each kind of plant, we must decide where we allow our mind to go or not to go, because we too will reap accordingly. But again, how much control *do* we have over the events in our ever-changing lives? We have the power to make decisions within the flow of cause and effect, but we cannot change the rules that give order to the universe. This *sūtra* is a reminder not to exaggerate our own importance by assuming we have powers that in fact lie beyond our reach.

4.4 **Calculated intentions [arise] from the ego alone.**

निर्माणचित्तान्यस्मितामात्रात् ॥

nirmāṇacittāny asmitāmātrāt

nirmāṇa: measure, measuring
citta: intention, aim, wish, thinking, reflecting, observing
asmitā: ego, egoity
mātra: only

The previous *sūtra* showed that resolution and nurturance are closely tied. The decisions we make and the actions we take are all designed to serve a purpose—our purpose. We do things for a reason and expect certain results. Where do our desires and our intentions to fulfill them come from? There is one source, and that is the human ego. Why? Because the ego creates a sense of separateness, limitation, and even alienation. Something is always lacking, and we are always trying to make up for that in one way or another.

4.5 **In all the ways that [a mind] is active, the mind that prompts [discipline] is one among many.**

प्रवृत्तिभेदे प्रयोजकं चित्तमेकमनेकेषाम्॥५॥

pravṛttibhede prayojakaṁ cittam ekam anekeṣām

pravṛtti: outward flow of consciousness into the world of multiplicity
bheda: difference, division, diversity, separation
prayojaka: causing, effecting, prompting, instigating
citta: mind, individual field of awareness
eka: one
aneka: many

Each mind is a unique center of awareness, colored by its own distinct thoughts, attitudes, and aspirations. That is why we each have our own unique experience of life. Rare indeed is the mind that chooses to turn away from the distracting enticements and excitement of the surrounding world in pursuit of an inner simplicity and quietude. Such a mind, even at the beginning of the spiritual journey, is one among many.

4.6 **There [in that mind], born of meditation, is the freedom from intention.**

तत्र ध्यानजमनाशयम् ॥

tatra dhyānajam anāśayam

tatra: there, therefore
dhyāna: meditation
ja: born
anāśaya: without thought, intention, or latent impressions

Cravings and intentions do not arise for one who is established in the mind's singular focus on its object. This state of awareness, called meditation, is likened to the uninterrupted flow of oil or honey poured from one vessel to another. There simply is no room for any other thought to arise or to form a desire or an impression leading to further bondage.

The traditional interpretation of *sūtras* 4.1–6, begun by Vyāsa and accepted by virtually every commentator or translator ever since, must not go unmentioned. Vyāsa believed that these six *sūtras* describe a *yogin*'s paranormal ability to create other bodies and other minds, because in *sūtra* 4.4 he took *cittāni* (the plural of *citta*) to mean multiple individual minds. However, *citta* in the sense of individual mind is a specialized meaning; the basic and more general meaning of *citta* is "intention," and the *sūtra* should be read as, "Calculated intentions [arise] from the ego alone"—not, as Vyāsa would have it, as "Created minds [are made from the *yogin's*] ego only." This weird misreading laid the foundation for ever more farfetched elaborations of yogically created minds and bodies as vehicles for the advanced practitioner's enjoyments as well as for the performance of rigorous austerities.

These six *sūtras* are not concerned with occult powers at all. Rather, they take us right back to the experience of our ordinary lives and the transformations we can effect to raise our level of attainment from the mundane to the spiritual.

4.7 **The actions of a *yogin* are neither black nor white, but those of others are of three kinds.**

कर्माशुक्लाकृष्णं योगिनस्त्रिविधमितरेषाम् ॥

karmāśuklākṛṣṇaṁ yoginas trividham itareṣām

karma: action and its consequences
aśukla: not white
akṛṣṇa: not black
yogin: practitioner of yoga
trividha: threefold, of three kinds
itara: other

Actions born of a purified consciousness do not stem from the ego's demands but rest above such need-driven activity. Such actions are neither good nor bad. Being neutral, they produce no results. Karma requires intent, but when one transcends the ego, what remains to produce intent?

For most of us, however, the situation is different. Our intentions and the actions that arise from them can be black (evil), white (good), or more likely mixed. In any case they will produce consequences accordingly, as the next *sūtra* observes.

4.8 **The tendencies they create will assuredly conform to how those [actions] come to fruition.**

ततस्तद्विपाकानुगुणानामेवाभिव्यक्तिर्वासनानाम् ॥

tatas tadvipākānuguṇānāṁ evābhivyaktir vāsanānām

tatas: from that (the three kinds of karma)
tad: those (actions and their consequences)
vipāka: ripening, maturing, effect, result, consequence of past or present action
anuguṇa: having similar qualities, according or suitable to, of the same nature, conformable to
eva: indeed, surely
abhivyakti: manifestation, distinction
vāsanā: subconscious impression, latent tendency, inclination

As you think, so you become; as you sow, so shall you reap. Every action, be it in thought, word, or deed, leaves its mark on the mind and is preserved as a subconscious impression. With repetition, the impressions become reinforced and deepen into ingrained tendencies. These in turn surface to influence how we think, speak, and act in the present, and that will have an effect on the future, for better or for worse. If we can manage our own thoughts, words, and deeds, we can have a say in the kinds of consequences they will eventually produce.

4.9 **Because latent impressions and memories are of a single nature, there is continuity [between them], even though [there may be] distance in time, place, and circumstance.**

जातिदेशकालव्यवहितानामप्यानन्तर्यं
स्मृतिसंस्कारयोरेकरूपत्वात् ॥

jātideśakālavyavahitānām apy ānantaryaṁ smṛtisaṁskārayor ekarūpatvāt

jāti: kind, category, type of birth
deśa: place
kāla: time
vyavahita: separate, noncontiguous, interrupted, placed apart, remote, distant
api: also, even though, although
ānantarya: immediate sequence, absence of interval, continuity
smṛti: memory
saṁskāra: latent impression
ekarūpatva: uniformity, the state of having one nature

Simply put, once an experience has impressed itself on the mind, it remains, whether lying there latent and undetected or resurfacing to active awareness as a revived memory.

Memory has a vital role to play. It gives continuity to our experience of life in more ways than one. Consider the basic act of perception. Without its memory bank the mind would have no content other than the experience of the moment, and it could not interpret much of that without anything to relate it to. How could you recognize a person, an object, a word, or anything else if the memory of previous experiences were not stored in the mind? And besides its role in the act of perception, the memory of a past moment, relived mentally, bridges the past and present, again providing continuity to life.

Now karma is a long-term proposition. While some actions produce immediate results, others take a long while to bear fruit; but they will bear fruit because the connection remains. Consequences will unfold at their own pace, even if that pace is glacial. That is why it is so difficult, even impossible, to know why some things happen or what makes us who and what we are. We simply cannot see a big enough picture to figure it all out, and our attempts are often futile.

4.10 **And the [impressions] are [said to be] beginningless, because the desire [to exist] is eternal.**

तासामनादित्वं चाशिसो नित्यत्वात् ॥

tāsām anāditvaṁ cāśiso nityatvāt

tāsām: of them (the tendencies)
anāditva: the state of having no beginning
ca: and
āśis: wish, desire, primordial will
nityatva: eternality, perpetuity, continual repetition

Once we have forgotten our true, original nature and identify as the finite ego-self, we cling to this mortal existence and all its involvements. Our recollection of a timeless state of being, empty of impressions, memories, or tendencies, has been obscured. In that sense all such tendencies are said to be beginningless.

All of India's philosophies see cosmic manifestation as an ever-repeating cycle of emergence, sustenance, and dissolution without beginning or end—a pulsation from the potential to the actual and back to the potential, only to be expressed again in another way. That is the divine play of being and becoming. Being is the eternally changeless reality of consciousness in itself; becoming is the actualizing in time and space of its inexhaustible possibilities. The human desire to exist is only a dim reflection of the supreme Self's desire for self-expression. As recorded in the Taittirīyopaniṣad (2.6.1):

> He [Brahman] desired, May I be many; may I grow forth. He deliberated, and having deliberated, he issued forth all this, whatever there is. Having issued it, he entered into it. Having entered into it, he became the present and the absent, the defined and the undefined, the settled and the unsettled, the sentient and the insentient, the true and the false. The reality [that is Brahman] became all this, whatever there is.

4.11 **Because impressions accumulate through [the process of] cause and effect and [the connection of] perception and its object, when these [factors] are negated, those [tendencies also] are negated.**

हेतुफलाश्रयालम्बनैः सङ्गृहीतत्वादेषामभावे तदभावः ॥

hetuphalāśrayālambanaiḥ saṅgṛhītatvād eṣām abhāve tadabhāvaḥ

hetu: cause
phala: effect
āśraya: that to which anything is closely connected or on which it depends; here, the object of perception
ālambana: seizure, taking hold of, touching; here, perception
saṅgṛhītatva: collection, accumulation
eṣām: of them
abhāva: absence, nonexistence, negation
tad: that (tendencies)
abhāva: absence. nonexistence, negation

The world as we know it is a vast web based on the principle of cause and effect and woven from everything we experience. Everything leaves an impression on the mind, unseen below the surface. Does this mean we are fated to be caught up forever in an unbreakable cycle of existence? No. Patañjali tells us that it is possible to break the connections, in effect to tear through the net so that it can no longer hold us.

4.12 **Past is past and future is future because of the differences of their characteristics.**

अतीतानागतं स्वरूपतोऽस्त्यध्वभेदाद्धर्माणाम् ॥

atītānāgataṁ svarūpato 'sty adhvabhedād dharmāṇām

atīta: past
anāgata: future
svarūpatas: by its own nature, according to its own form
asti: is
adhvan: road, way, journey, course, orbit, time
bheda: difference, distinction
dharma: characteristic, property, quality, distinctive condition

Our existence seems driven by time, so what is time? What is the difference between something I did yesterday, something I am doing today, and something I will do tomorrow? The past is that which has already been experienced and is stored in my mind as a memory; the present is that which occupies my mind now; the future is that which I have yet to experience and is present to my mind only as an expectation. I and my experience are the factors of all three states but in different ways, because time is a reality of constant change

4.13 **Those [characteristics, both] visible and intangible, have the nature of the [three] elemental forces.**

ते व्यक्तसूक्ष्मा गुणात्मानः ॥

te vyaktasūkṣmā guṇātmānaḥ

te: those (characteristics)
vyakta: visible, evident, perceptible by the senses
sūkṣma; subtle, intangible, fine
guṇātman: having the nature (*ātman*) of the forces of creation (*guṇa*: one of the three universal energies—clarity/repose [*sattva*], passion/restlessness [*rajas*], and obscuration/inertia [*tamas*])

Everything that is manifest in the past, the present, or the future is composed of the same building blocks, the three elemental forces of creation. This is an idea we met earlier in *sūtra* 2.19.

4.14 **The distinctiveness of [any] object [arises] from the uniting [of the elemental forces] in the [course of] transformation.**

परिणामैकत्वाद्वस्तुतत्त्वम् ॥

pariṇāmaikatvād vastutattvam

pariṇāma: transformation, change
ekatva: oneness, unity, union, coincidence, identity
vastu: object, thing, article
tattva: "thatness," essence, elementary property, reality

We live in a universe filled with objects, and those objects are of two kinds. One kind is made of physical matter. It has form and color, weight and texture, perhaps flavor, odor, and sound. When awareness of such an object and its qualities becomes present to the mind, we call that perception.

The other kind of object is intangible. It is a thought, an emotion, an idea, a concept. Nevertheless, it too becomes present to the mind and forms part of our experience. All of human life is an interaction with both kinds of objects—the physical and the mental. All of them, whatever they are, are shaped by the three elemental forces of creation.

As the Sāṁkhya philosophy explains, *prakṛti* is the primordial source of the manifest universe. Within it are the three basic forces of creation, known as the *guṇas* ("threads" or "qualities"). When these are in perfect equilibrium, creation is unmanifest, existing only in a potential state. Owing to the proximity of *puruṣa,* the conscious principle, the balance is upset, and the *guṇas* are set in motion, combining and recombining to produce everything in the universe from the highest insight of human intelligence to the insentient density of a stone. A similar idea is found in modern physics, where two classes of elementary particles (material and force-carrying) interact through four fundamental forces (gravitational, electromagnetic, strong nuclear, and weak nuclear), producing all the phenomena that make up the universe.

4.15 **[But even] when the object is the same, it is perceived in different ways, because [individual] minds are different.**

वस्तुसाम्ये चित्तभेदात्तयोर्विभक्तः पन्थाः ॥

vastusāmye cittabhedāt tayor vibhaktaḥ panthāḥ

vastu: object
sāmya: sameness
citta: individual mind
bheda: distinction, difference, separation
tayoḥ: of the two (the object and the mind)

vibhakta: parting, separation, difference
panthan: way, course, path

Here Patañjali shifts the perspective. He has been exploring the nature of things that exist. Now he turns our attention to the question of how we know them.

A large audience will see a film, but no two people will experience it in exactly the same way. One might find it engrossing, another tiresome, one excellent, another disappointing. In the same way, one person viewing a garden may find it beautiful while another will see much room for improvement. One likes roses; another prefers carnations. Every person experiences the world through an individual mind and sees through a different set of lenses or filters. Each mind is colored by the entire store of impressions from the past, shaping its likes and dislikes, its attitudes and convictions, and every other nuance that makes that person's experience unique and unlike any other. What this *sūtra* aims to say is that we all see the same natural phenomena—the same sun, moon, sky, earth, trees, buildings, people, and so on, as well as the same events—yet for each of us they are different because each of *us* is different.

4.16 **Nor does the object depend on [the perception of] a single mind. If the object were not perceived by it, then would it exist?**

च चैकचित्ततन्त्रम्चेद्वस्तु तदप्रमाणकं तदा किं स्यात् ॥

na caikacittatantraṁ ced vastu tadapramāṇakaṁ tadā kiṁ syāt

na: not
ca: and
eka: one
citta: mind
tantra: dependent on
ced: if
vastu: object

tad: it (the mind)
apramāṇaka: imperceptible, not cognized
tadā: then
kim: (interrogative particle)
syāt: it would exist

Patañjali wishes to make two points here. The first is that the existence of an object does not depend on its being perceived by any single mind. Recall the teaching of *sūtra* 2.22 that an object of experience vanishes from one mind even while continuing in the shared experience of others.

The second part of the *sūtra* is a philosophical question, and if it seems jarring here, it was meant to be. There are those thinkers, called philosophical idealists, who believe that an object exists *only* in one's perception of it. And there are others, called realists, who believe that objects exist independently. Philosophers of both persuasions will argue back and forth until they are blue in the face, but in the end, do they resolve anything? The question remains, to be revisited over and over.

So what is Patañjali's point? To show how eagerly the mind gets caught up in its thoughts and fails to recognize its own true nature. We do not see the forest for the trees.

4.17 **Because the coloration of that [object] is needed, an object is either known or not known to the mind.**

तदुपरागापेक्षित्वाच्चित्तस्य वस्तु ज्ञाताज्ञातम् ॥

taduparāgāpekṣitvāc cittasya vastu jñātājñātam

tad: that (object)
uparāga: coloration, influence
apekṣitva: necessity
citta: individual mind
vastu: object, thing
jñāta: known
ajñāta: not known

The object does exist apart from the mind. It has its own distinctive qualities, and when they color the mind, as a nearby object appears to color a crystal (the illustration given in *sūtra* 1.41), then knowledge of the object occurs. If there is no coloration, no knowledge of the object is present to the mind at that time. But that is not the whole story, as we will learn next.

4.18 **The modifications of the mind are always known by something greater [than itself], because of the unchanging nature of consciousness.**

सदा ज्ञाताश्चित्तवृत्तयस्तत्प्रभोः
पुरुषस्यापरिणामित्वात् ॥

sadā jñātāś cittavṛttayas tatprabhoḥ
puruṣasyāpariṇāmitvāt

sadā: always
jñāta: known
citta: individual mind
vṛtti: fluctuation, activity, midification
tad: that
prabhu: more powerful than, having power over, constant; master, lord
puruṣa: consciousness, the higher Self
apariṇāmitva: immutability, changelessness

It is through the activities of the mind that we think our knowledge arises—through the modifications that reflect the outward things we perceive and through the inner ideas that take shape within our own awareness. But what is it that allows us to know *them?*

There is something greater than the mind, always present regardless of whatever else comes momentarily to our notice and then just as quickly departs. That is the steady, unchanging light of consciousness itself, by which all else is known.

4.19 **[The mind] is not self-luminous because it is [a] visible [object of perception].**

न तत्स्वाभासम्दृश्यत्वात् ॥

na tat svābhāsam dṛśyatvāt

na: not
tad: it (the mind)
svābhāsa: self-luminous
dṛśyatva: visibility

If it is difficult to think of the mind as an object, consider that you can—and do—think about your own mind, you observe its activities and moods, and you speak of it as *your* mind. Doesn't that hint at its objective nature?

The sun shines by its own light, but the moon's soft glow is the reflected light of the sun. In the same way, the supreme Self shines by its own light as the pure subject. The mind, existing in nature, has the status of an object and appears to shine, but in truth it only reflects the light of the Self.

4.20 **It is not possible to think of both [the mind and the supreme consciousness] at the same time.**

एकसमये चोभयानवधारणम् ॥

ekasamaye cobhayānavadhāraṇam

ekasamaye: at the same time
ca: and
ubhaya: both
anavadhāraṇa: nonascertaiunment, nonaffirmation, nonreflection

It is impossible to be simultaneously bound and liberated. Let us recall what Patañjali set out at the beginning of his instruction. Immediately after announcing the presentation of yoga, he disclosed in the following three *sūtras* (1.2–4) that yoga is the absolute stilling of the mind's activity; that to achieve this is to abide in one's own true nature; and that otherwise one identifies as a small and separate self and experiences the everchanging world through the mind's ongoing activity.

We become totally intrigued by all of the sights, sounds, smells, tastes, and touches of the world around us. Then by our responses to them and by our ideas and feelings concerning those responses, we become so caught up with these contents of consciousness that we fail to be aware of consciousness itself. To repeat what was said a short while ago, we do not see the forest for the trees.

4.21 **If one mind could see into another, one [human] intelligence would go beyond engagement with another, and [their] memories [would become] intermixed.**

चित्तान्तरदृश्ये बुद्धिबुद्धेरतिप्रसङ्गः स्मृतिसङ्करश्च ॥

cittāntaradṛśye buddhibuddher atiprasaṇgaḥ
smṛtisaṅkaraś ca

citta: individual mind
antara: another
dṛśya: seeing, perception
buddhi: intelligence, the highest function of the human mind
atiprasaṇga: excessive connection
smṛti: memory
saṅkara: confusion, intermxing
ca: and

The whole point of human "I-am-ness" is that each of us is a distinct individual with a distinct history, a distinct constitution, and a distinct destiny.

Recall that in *sūtra* 3.19 Patañjali informed us that "through [full comprehension] of the contents of one's own mind [arises] knowledge of the minds of others." In the very next *sūtra* he added, "But *not* of the content of another's mind, since that is not the object [of one's own] mind." Now he gives a deeper insight into that. If one person could experience the thoughts of another as vividly as if they were one's own, those thoughts would leave their mark in the form of indelible impressions, and two individual minds—two separate spheres of consciousness—would become hopelessly entangled with a shared mixture of past and present experience, which would in turn influence the future. Another's actions would become my, or your, karma. Each personality is separate for a reason.

4.22 **Because consciousness [itself] remains unmixed [with anything else], when forms take shape within it, the perception is that of its own power of thought.**

चितेरप्रतिसङ्क्रमायास्तदाकारापत्तौ स्वबुद्धिसंवेदनम् ॥

citer apratisaṅkramāyās tadākārāpattau svabuddhi-saṁvedanam

citi: consciousness in its creative aspect
apratisaṅkrama: having no intermixture
tad: that, it
ākāra: form, figure, shape, appearance
āpatti: occurence, happening, entering into a state or condition, changing into
sva: own
buddhi: the power of forming and retaining conceptions, intelligence
saṁvedana: the act of perceiving, perception

Here Patañjali hints at a higher awareness. Just as the sun's rays are not altered by the objects that they illuminate but remain as the pure nature of light, so the consciousness that is the higher Self remains just that—the light of awareness that makes all things knowable without actually being altered by them.

And here Patañjali lets us in on a secret. All the forms that take shape in the mind are of the essence of consciousness itself, and consciousness remains eternally unmixed. It is what it is, pure and simple. Think of a glass of ice water. The ice cubes appear as distinct objects floating in the water. Each has its own size and shape and a unique pattern of bubbles and clouding or the clarity of having no bubbles at all. But in essence the ice cubes are nothing other than water, only appearing for a while to have form and characteristics.

4.23 **The mind that is colored by [the distinction] of the seer and the seen [can know] all objects.**

द्रष्टृदृश्योपरक्तं चित्तं सर्वार्थम् ॥

dṛaṣṭṛdṛśyoparaktaṁ cittaṁ sarvārtham

dṛaṣṭṛ: seer
dṛśya: the seen, the visible
uparakta: dyed, colored, afflicted, distressed
citta: individual mind
sarvārtha: suitable for every purpose, aim, or objective

Sūtra 4.20 taught that it is not possible to think of both the mind and the supreme consciousness at the same time. That is because supreme consciousness is not—and can never be—an object of thought. It is that by which thought becomes possible.

In any act of perceiving or thinking, there must be a knower and something to be known, and these two exist relative to each other. They depend on each other. How can you speak of a knower if there is nothing to know? And how can you speak of something as known if there is no knower?

The distinction of subject and object arises and exists solely within consciousness itself. These two factors (along with the process or act of knowing that relates them) have to be present in the individual mind in order for it to interact with the world in all its diversity, in order for it to have the full range of human experience.

4.24 **The mind, colored by countless latent tendencies, comes to depend on things other than itself owing to its interaction [with them].**

तदसङ्ख्येयवासनाचित्रमपि परार्थं संहत्यकारित्वात् ॥

tadasaṅkhyeyavāsanācitram api parārthaṁ saṁhatyakāritvāt

tad: that (mind)
asaṅkhyeya: uncountable

vāsanā: impressions, tendencies
citra: variegated
api: also, moreover, besides, surely, even
parārtha: dependent on something else
saṁhatya: joined, combined, working together with
kāritva: activity

The mind, forgetful of the true Self as consciousness itself, becomes colored, distracted, and dependent on things that appear different from itself. It falls into the state of human bondage and, through the force of habit, gets stuck there. The question becomes, how do we break free?

4.25 **For one who distinguishes [between the knowing subject and the known object], the mental production of the individual's sense of self comes to an end.**

विशेषदर्शिन आत्मभावभावनाविनिवृत्तिः ॥

viśeṣadarśina ātmabhāvabhāvanāvinivṛttiḥ

viśeṣa: distinction, particularity
darśin: seer
ātman: self
bhāva: state of existence
bhāvanā: the act of producing, a forming in the mind, mental formulation, imagination, conception
vinivṛtti: cessation, coming to an end, discontinuance

We have created our own personal identities by associating with things and factors that lie outside of our true being and by claiming we are made of them or possess them. I am this body, I am this mind, I am my likes and dislikes, my talents and abilities, my hopes and fears. But in truth I am not. I, the eternal subject, am not any of those objects with which I identify. While everything about me and my world is constantly changing, I am in truth the unchanging witness, eternally free.

Here is that same idea, expressed over a thousand years ago by Abhinavagupta, an illumined seer of the Kashmiri Śaiva tradition, in his *Twelve Verses on the Highest Truth:*

Let accumulating time drive the moments onward;
let the creator assiduously create, or let a passion compelled by another lead to sore distress.
Let these come about through the external sound and fury of the cosmic play or through the internal doings of the embodied soul, whose ongoing flow of ever-shifting self-definition seems as if founded on air. In this constantly changing, grand delusion, am I not a spectator?

4.26 **Then the mind, immersed in discernment, becomes inclined toward liberation.**

तदा विवेकनिम्नं कैवल्यप्राग्भारं चित्तम् ॥

tadā vivekanimnaṁ kaivalyaprāgbhāraṁ cittam

tadā: then
viveka: discernment, discrimination
nimna: inclined toward, deep, immersed
kaivalya: perfect isolation of consciousness from matter (Sāṁkhya definition); absolute unity, singularity (Advaita Vedānta definition); liberation
prāgbhāra: inclination, propensity
citta: individual mind

Recall again that we either abide in our own true nature or that we identify as small and separate selves that experience the ever-changing world through the mind's activity. In *sūtra* 4.20 Patañjali taught that we experience the one or the other and that it is not possible to experience the two at the same time. There is, however, a point of transition, and practicing the mental discernment of Self and not-self takes us in that direction. The more mindful we become, the more inclined we are toward the right understanding that leads to liberation.

4.27 **With interruptions of [that discerning state] other thoughts [rise up] because of latent impressions.**

तच्छिद्रेषु प्रत्ययान्तराणि संस्कारेभ्यः ॥

tacchidreṣu pratyayāntarāṇi saṁskārebhyaḥ

tad: that
chidra: cut, slit, tear, cleft, opening, defect, fault, blemish, imperfection, weakness
pratyaya: idea, conception, anything present to awareness
antara: other
saṁskāra: latent impression

At this point we may begin to see the forest for the trees, but only in momentary flashes. Our experiences of a higher state of consciousness—of a higher state of being—will at first be only intermittent, and between those rare moments, back in the long stretches of ordinary awareness, we are once more subject to the vast store of impressions that are ready to rise up again. We are not out of the woods yet—not until we become fully established in the knowledge of the higher Self.

4.28 **Getting rid of these [impressions] is said to be like [getting rid of] the causes of distress.**

हानमेषां क्लेशवदुक्तम् ॥

hānam eṣāṁ kleśavad uktam

hāna: act of abandoning, relinquishing, giving up, getting rid of, cessation
eṣām: of these
kleśavad: like the causes of distress
ukta: said

In *sūtra* 2.3 Patañjali taught that there are five causes of human distress or affliction, which he identified as ignorance of our true being, identification with the ego, the attractions that draw the mind, the aversions that repel it, and the patterns of habit and behavior into which we fall. *Sūtra* 2.10 taught that the way to overcome these five causes of human bondage is to reverse the flow of consciousness. The same principle is true of even the most subtle buried impressions. Should we see them begin to arise, the trick is not to allow the mind to follow them to where they can play out but rather to direct our awareness back to beyond where they originate—back to the pure, untouched consciousness that is our core being. It is a matter of reversing the flow of consciousness—away from its contents and back to itself.

4.29 **For one who gives up expectation of even [the highest rewards of] meditation, whose vision is [one of pure] discernment in every way, [there arises] a meditative union clouded [only] by virtue.**

प्रसङ्ख्यानेऽप्यकुसीदस्य सर्वथा विवेकख्यातेर् धर्ममेघः समाधिः ॥

prasaṅkhyāne 'py akusīdasya sarvathā vivekakhyāter dharmameghaḥ samādhiḥ

prasaṅkhyāna: reflection, deep meditation, renown, payment, liquidation of a debt
api: also, moreover, besides, surely, even
akusīda: taking no interest in gain, nonusurious
sarvathā: in every way, in every respect, altogether, entirely, at all times
vivekakhyāti: one whose perception or knowledge is discernment or discrimination
dharma: virtue
megha: cloud
samādhi: meditative union, unitary consciousness

To aspire to anything is to admit a lack of fulfillment. To aspire to spiritual perfection is to acknowledge that it remains to be attained. This is a truth evasive in its simplicity. One who is truly discerning recognizes this, and one who becomes established in that discernment becomes completely dispassionate and free of self-interest.

But remember that the supreme goal of yoga is the complete stilling of the mind's activity, and even the highest dis-

> cernment is still a form of mental activity and not the state of abiding in one's true being as consciousness devoid of all objective content and whole in its own crystalline purity. At this point the mind is like a crystal still clouded by a trace of content—and that content or reflection is discernment itself. That is why this advanced state of meditative absorption is described as "clouded [only] by virtue."

The interpretation proposed here rests on a strict grammatical reading and the context of the surrounding *sūtras*. It represents a break with established tradition.

The explanation involves some technicalities of Sanskrit syntax. *Vivekakhyāteḥ* is an adjectival (*bahuvrīhi*) compound in the masculine genitive singular; it means "of one whose vision or knowledge is discernment." It refers to the same person who is also free of expectation even for the highest attainment (*akusīda*). For such a person, in a state of utter desirelessness, there arises a state of meditative absorption described as *dharmamegha*. This term is also a *bahuvrīhi* compound; it means "whose cloud is *dharma*," "*dharma*-clouded," or "clouded by *dharma*." According to this reading, *dharmamegha samādhi* is a state in which all that remains to cloud pure consciousness is *dharma* itself. And what is that? The word *dharma* has no exact English counterpart; its many meanings include "virtue," "righteousness," "merit," "morality," "prescribed conduct," "duty," "character," or "essential quality."

The term *dharmamegha* is all but unknown in Hindu tradition, and the classical commentators and their modern successors all seem unsure of what to make of it. Our reading of it as an adjectival (*bahuvrīhi*) compound is unique; Vyāsa and all the others take it as a *tatpuruṣa* compound, translated as "cloud of *dharma*," "cloud of virtue," or "cloud of merit," in apposition to *samādhi*.

Vyāsa's commentary points out that the state of highest and constant dispassion allows for nothing further to become present to the mind, but he does not even attempt to explain what *dharmamegha samādhi* might mean. Bryant (pp. 450–452) writes that the commentators understand it generally as the highest state of discrimination, but from there each draws a different conclusion. According to a commentary attributed to the Advaita Vedānta philosopher Śaṁkarācārya (788–820) but not authenticated, the *dharma* rained by this cloud is *kaivalya,* or ultimate liberation—the resting of the supreme Self (*puruṣa*) in the serenity of its own desirelessness. A generation later Vācaspati Miśra took *dharmamegha samādhi* to signify supreme dispassion toward any manifest thing. For Vijñānabhikṣu, in the fifteenth century, it meant the state of liberation while living (*jīvanmukti*); like a cloud that gives rain, the cloud of *dharma* rains the purifying virtue that destroys the causes of suffering and the bondage of karma. In sharp contrast a Vedāntin of the sixteenth century, Rāmānanda Sarasvatī, took *dharma* to signify "all knowable things" and the "cloud of *dharma samādhi*" as the state of knowing all knowable things. For Hariharānanda Āraṇya (1869–1947) *dharmamegha samādhi* meant an omniscience arising from discrimination whereby the *yogin* sees even his highest attainments as suffering (*duḥkha*); Hariharānanda also understood *dharma* as "virtue" and envisioned this kind of *samādhi* as raining the highest virtue, which includes Self-knowledge.

Apart from the *Yogasūtra* the term *dharmamegha samādhi* occurs in only one other Hindu text, the *Paiṅgalopaniṣad* (3.2). This is a late Upaniṣad that combines elements of the Vedānta philosophy with the fully developed ideas of classical Sāṁkhya and references to yogic practice. In all likelihood it is later than the *Yogasūtra.* The teaching, attributed to the ancient seer Yājñavalkya, goes like this: the *yogin* is to meditate on the thought "I am Brahman" with absolute one-pointedness until the steadiness of meditation becomes like that of a lamp-flame, unflickering in a windless place (an analogy borrowed from the Bhagavadgītā). When all active cognizing ceases, the web of impressions accumulated through countless lifetimes begins to dissolve, and a stream of nectar (which is to say the Self's inherent bliss) showers forth in a thousand directions. "Therefore the adepts in yoga call this highest attainment 'the cloud of virtue.' ... Then one becomes liberated while living" (*tato yogavittamāḥ samādhiṁ dharmameghaṁ prāhuḥ ... tadā jīvanmukto bhavati*). It is quite possible that this passage is a reference to the text of the *Yogasūtra.* It appears to have influenced some of the later commentators, but there is little reason to think that it conveys what Patañjali might have meant.

It must be noted also that the term *dharmamegha samādhi* occurs with some frequency in the Buddhist Mahāyāna tradition. In the *Daśabhūmikasūtra,* dating from the early third century and therefore roughly contemporary with Patañjali, the term signifies the highest level of attainment for the *boddhisattva,* a soul who forgoes liberation and, out of compassion, accepts rebirth in order to work for the liberation of others. Whether or not that was what Patañjali had in mind we will never know. However, this definition seems out of context with the *Yogasūtra*'s emphasis on the individual's liberation.

4.30 **After that, [human] affliction and the [bondage of actions and their consequences] cease.**

ततः क्लेशकर्मनिवृत्तिः ॥

tataḥ kleśakarmanivṛttiḥ

tatas: from there, thereupon, thence, consequently
kleśa: affliction, existential distress
karma: karma
nivṛtti: cessation

In full spiritual illumination the light of truth shines so brightly that everything else dissolves in the brilliance. Whatever we see in ordinary awareness—all the forms and colors—consist of light and shadow, but when there is only light, then there is only light—the light of our own higher, transcendental awareness.

4.31 **Then, because of the unlimited knowledge [that ensues], for one who is free from all the coverings and limitations [of awareness], little [remains] to be known.**

तदा सर्वावरणमलापेतस्य
ज्ञानस्यानन्त्याज्ज्ञेयमल्पम् ॥

tadā sarvāvaraṇamalāpetasya jñānasyānantyāj jñeyam alpam

tadā: then
sarva: all
āvaraṇa: covering, concealing, hiding, obstruction, enclosing

mala: dirt, impurity, limitation
āpeta: free from
jñāna: knowledge
ānantya: endlessness, infinity
jñeya: to be known
alpa: little

Little remains to be known? How about *nothing* remains to be known? Why the understatement? Because Patañjali knows that the ultimate truth is inexpressible and that no utterance, however grand, can even begin to tell us what enlightenment is like. We have to experience it for ourselves, and then, in the fullness of that knowledge, we are silent.

4.32 **Consequently there comes about a complete end to the sequence of the transformations of the elemental forces, whose purpose has been fulfilled.**

ततः कृतार्थानां परिणामक्रमपरिसमाप्तिर्गुणानाम् ॥

tataḥ kṛtārthānāṁ pariṇāmakramaparisamāptir guṇānām

tatas: from there, thereupon, thence, consequently
kṛta: done, accomplished, filfilled
artha: purpose
pariṇāma: transformation, change
krama: sequence
parisamāpti: complete conclusion, end
guṇa: elemental force

In this silence there is no change. The activity of the forces of creation comes to an end, having fulfilled its purpose, which was the dynamic experience of embodied human existence.

4.33 **Sequence is associated with the moments [in time] and can be perceived until the very end of change.**

क्षणप्रतियोगी परिणामापरान्तनिर्ग्राह्यः क्रमः ॥

kṣaṇapratiyogī pariṇāmāparāntanirgrāhyaḥ kramaḥ

kṣaṇa: instant
pratiyogin: any object depending on another and having no independent existence; partner, associate
pariṇāma: transformation
aparānta: extreme end
nirgrāhya: perceivable, to be traced or found out
krama: sequence, succession

Without change there is no time, and without time there is no change. The two cannot exist without each other, nor can they exist without sequence. The experience of the world depends on this. When all differentiated mental activity stops, there ceases to be any change in consciousness. Along with the effects of change, the progression of change—the concept of sequence—itself vanishes. In the absence of sequence, there is only timelessness, eternal and unchanging. That is the experience of the supreme Self.

4.34 **[When] the forces of creation, devoid of purpose for the supreme Self, return to their original state, [that is known as] the singularity [of liberation] or the power of consciousness established in its own nature.**

पुरुषार्थशून्यानां गुणानां प्रतिप्रसवः कैवल्यं
स्वरूपप्रतिष्ठा वा चितिशक्तिरिति ॥

puruṣārthaśūnyānāṁ guṇānāṁ pratiprasavaḥ kaivalyaṁ svarūpapratiṣṭhā vā citiśaktir iti

puruṣa: consciousness, the Self
artha: purpose, aim, intent
śūnya: empty, devoid of
guṇa: elemental force
pratiprasava: return to the original state
kaivalya: isolation, perfect detachment, beatitude, absolute unity
svarūpa: own form, essence
pratiṣṭha: established
vā: or

citi: consciousness
śakti: power, energy
iti: thus

It is highly significant that Patañjali ends his magisterial treatise on yoga with not one but two definitions of liberation. This reaffirms what is implicit in his opening declaration: his indebtedness to the many yogic traditions that preceded him.

The definition of liberation or enlightenment as *kaivalya* reflects the Sāṁkhya view. Once consciousness (*puruṣa*) has been completely disentangled from matter (*prakṛti*), the elemental energies of creation (*guṇas*) cease their activity. There is no reason for them to continue; the true Self (*puruṣa*) has no purpose, so there is no purpose they could assume for its sake. *Kaivalya* means "aloneness" or "isolation," and in the classic Sāṁkhya view, liberation or enlightenment is the total disengagement of subjective consciousness from involvement with anything of an objective or material nature. The word *kaivalya* can also be taken in the Vedantic sense as absolute unity, the experience of the infinite, transcendental Brahman.

But then Patañjali gives a second definition of the supreme goal, which he calls "the power of consciousness established in its own nature." The words *citi* and *śakti* both have a strong Tantric Śaiva resonance. *Citi* denotes consciousness as a dynamic reality, vibrantly alive in its own being, and the presence of the word *śakti* affirms that consciousness and its power are indeed a single and singular reality.

The ultimate truth is, of course, beyond all attempts to describe it. It is the reality that remains, self-luminous, when all activity of the mind has been stilled.

Selected References

Bryant, Edwin F. *The Yoga Sūtras of Patañjali: With Insights from the Traditional Commentators.* New York: North Point Press, 2009.

Dvivedi, M. N. *The Yoga-Sūtras of Patañjali.* 1890. Reprint. Delhi: Sri Satguru Publications, 2001.

Feuerstein, Georg. *The Yoga-Sūtra of Patañjali: A New Translation and Commentary.* Rochester, VT: Inner Traditions International, 1989.

Kālī, Devadatta. *Śvetāśvataropaniṣad: The Knowledge That Liberates.* Lake Worth, FL: Nicolas Hays, 2011.

Larson, Gerald James. *Classical Sāṁkhya: An Interpretation of Its History and Meaning.* 2nd ed. Delhi: Motilal Banarsidass, 1979.

Nicholson, Andrew J. *Unifying Hinduism: Philosophy and Identity in Indian Intellectual History.* New York: Columbia University Press, 2010.

Pandey, Kanti Chandra. *An Outline of History of Śaiva Philosophy.* 1954. Reprint. Delhi: Motilal Banarsidass, 1999.

Prabhavananda, Swami, and Isherwood, Christopher. *How to Know God: The Yoga Aphorisms of Patanjali.* Hollywood: Vedanta Press, 1953.

Prasāda, Rāma. *Patañjali's Yoga Sūtras: with the commentary of Vyāsa and the gloss of Vāchaspati Miśra.* 1912. Reprint. New Delhi: Munshiram Manoharlal, 2002.

Thematic Index by Sūtra

accomplishments, 4.1–6
activity of the mind, 1.2, 1.4–6, 2.11
apathy, 1.30
ardent discipline, 2.1, 2.32, 2.43, 4.1, 4.5
association (of subject and object), 2.23–24, 3.9
attraction, 2.3, 2.7
authority, 1.7
aversion, 2.3, 2.8
avoidance of excess, 2.30–31, 2.39

birth, circumstances of, 4.1–2
body, 3.42, 3.45–46
breath, 1.31, 1.34
breath control, 2.29, 2.49–51

calmness, 1.33
causality, 3.14, 4.11
change/transformation, 3.15, 4.2, 4.14, 4.32–33
characteristic, 3.13, 4.12–14
chastity, 2.30–31, 2.38
clarity, 1.33
compassion, 1.33, 3.23
concentration, 1.30, 2.29, 2.53, 3.1, 3.7–8
condition, 3.13
consciousness, 4.18, 4.20, 4.22
consciousness, power of, 4.34
content of the mind, 3.19–20
contentment, 2.32, 2.41
convergence (of mind and object), 1.41–44, 1.46–47
conviction, 1.20
crystal, 1.41
cultivation of opposites, 2.33–34, 2.42

death, 1.19
desire/will to live, 4.10
despondency, 1.31
detachment, 3.39
determination, 1.21–22
discernment, 2.26, 3.49, 3.52–54, 4.25, 4.29
dispassion, 1.12, 1.15–16, 3.50
distraction, 1.30–32, 3.11
distress, five causes of, 2.2–4, 2.10, 2.12, 4.28

dissipation, 1.30
"divine hearing," 3.41
doubt, 1.30
dream, 1.38

eight-limbed yoga, 2.27–3.8
elemental forces, 2.18–19, 4.13–14, 4.32, 4.34
endeavor, 1.12–14, 1.17
ego, 2.3, 2.6, 4.25
equanimity, 1.33, 3.23
expansion of self, 3.38, 3.40, 3.43
expectation, 4.30
experience of the world, 2.18, 2.22, 3.35, 3.44

flow of consciousness, 2.10
form, 3.13
"fourth, the," 2.51
freedom from limitation, 4.31

Great Vow, 2.31

habit, 2.3, 2.9
heart, 3.34
human condition, 3.45–47, 4.30

ideation, 1.6, 1.9
ignorance, 2.3–5, 2.24–26
illness, 1.30
impressions/latent tendencies, 1.18–19, 1.24, 1.50–51, 3.10, 3.18, 4.8–9, 4.11, 4.24, 4.27
inference, 1.7
insight, 1.20
instability, 1.30

karma, 2.12–14, 3.22, 4.7–9
kindness, 1.33, 3.23
knower-knowing-known, 1.41, 4.25

language, 1.42, 3.17
laziness, 1.30
liberation, 1.51, 3.50, 3.54, 4.34

manifestation, 3.9
meditation, 2.11, 2.29, 3.2, 3.7–8
meditative absorption/union, 1.20, 1.46, 1.51, 2.2, 2.29, 3.3, 3.7–8, 3.11, 4.1, 4.6
memory, 1.6, 1.11, 1.43
mental focus, 1.32, 1.35–40, 3.11
mind, as object, 4.19–20
mind, coloration of, 1.41, 4.17, 4.23–24
mindfulness, 1.20
mindfulness of the sacred, 2.1, 2.32, 2.45 (*see also* Supreme Being)
mind-reading, 3.20, 4.21
misapprehension, 1.6, 1.8, 1.30
misery, 1.31
moment, 3.52
moon, 3.27

navel, 3.29
negligence, 1.30
non-stealing, 2.30–31, 2.37
nonviolence, 2.30–31, 2.35
nurturance, 4.1, 4.3

objectivity, 1.45
obstacles, 1.29–30
OM, 1.27–28, 3.17
omnipotence, 3.49–50
omniscience, 3.33, 3.49–50, 4.31
opposites, 2.48

perceiver-perceiving-perceived, 2.6, 2.17, 2.20–24, 4.11, 4.23 (*see also* knower-knowing-known)
perception, 1.7, 3.13, 3.21, 3.25, 4.15–17, 4.22
polestar, 3.28
posture, 2.29, 2.46–48
purity, 2.32, 2.40

radiance, spiritual, 3.32
resolution, 4.1, 4.4
right knowledge, 1.6–7
right observances, 2.29, 2.32

sameness, 3.12
seedless meditative union, 1.51, 3.8
Self, 1.3, 1.16, 2.5, 3.49, 3.55, 4.34
self-aggrandizement, 3.51
self-restraint, 2.29–30
senses, 3.36–37, 3.47
sequence, 3.15, 3.52–54, 4.32–33
sleep, 1.6, 1.10, 1.38
space, 3.42
steadiness of mind, 1.35, 3.31
stilling of the mind, 1.2, 1.12, 1.13, 1.20, 1.23, 3.9, 4.27–28
stillness, 3.48
study, 2.1, 2.32, 2.44
suffering, 2.15–17
sun, 3.26
Supreme Being, 1.23–26

thought, rising and falling of, 3.12
throat, 3.30
time, 3.14, 3.16, 4.12, 4.33
"tortoise shell," 3.31
total engagement/full comprehension, 3.4–6, 3.16–17, 3.19, 3.21, 3.23–24, 3.26–31, 3.41–42, 3.44, 3.47, 3.52
trembling, 1.31
truth, 1.48
truthfulness, 2.30–31, 2.36

unity, 1.45, 1.49, 1.51, 4.34

veiling of consciousness, 2.52, 3.43
vigor, 1.20
virtue, 1.33, 3.23
"virtue-clouded" meditative union, 4.29

withdrawal of senses, 2.29, 2.54–55

yoga, 1.1–2
yoga of action, 2.1–2

About the Author

Devadatta Kālī (David Nelson) began his decades-long association with Hinduism in 1966 through the Vedanta Society of Southern California in Hollywood. He received initiation from Swami Prabhavananda three years later. A resident of Santa Barbara, he is active as a speaker at temples, ashrams, churches, colleges, and interfaith venues throughout Southern California.